RYA
Start to Race

Written by Jeremy Evans

© 2009 Jeremy Evans
Copyright RYA 2009
First Published 2009

The Royal Yachting Association
RYA House, Ensign Way
Hamble, Southampton
Hampshire SO31 4YA

Tel: 0845 345 0400
Fax: 0845 345 0329
E-mail: publications@rya.org.uk
Web: www.rya.org.uk

ISBN 978-1-905104-80-2
Order Code G66

Acknowledgements

Jeremy Evans would like to thank the following for their help. Minorca Sailing Holidays (www.minorcasailing.co.uk) for providing facilities for dinghy sequences at their wonderful centre on Fornells Bay. Cobnor Activities Centre (www.cobonor.com) for providing additional facilities for dinghy photos. Martin Wadhams and the team at LDC Racing Sailboats (www.ldcracingsailboats.co.uk) for help with images, illustrations and advice. Steve Cockerill of Rooster Sailing (www.roostersailing.com) for advice on single-handed dinghies. Pete Galvin for creating such beautiful, accurate illustrations. Steve Cockerill, Andy Taylor, Phil Sparks, Nick Craig and Frances Peters for their insights on what helps champions to win. Michael McNamara (www.mcnamara-sails.com) for his insight into coaching. Skandia Team GBR (www.skandiateamgbr.com) for providing Richard Langdon's stunning images. Trevor Lewis (author of the RYA Racing Rules Handbook and Going By The Rules) who provided a great deal of help with the new racing rules. And of course the RYA (www.rya.org.uk) for doing such a fantastic job in promoting dinghy racing and making their knowledge and back-up available.

Photo Credits

Jeremy Evans: 12, 13, 14, 15, 16, 17, 18, 19, 20, 21, 22, 23, 24 left, 25, 26 top, 27, 28, 29, 31, 32, 33, 41, 44, 50, 57, 58 top, 59, 60, 61, 64 bottom right, 65 top right, 73, 75 bottom, 81, 85, 86 top, 87, 91, 92, 93 top, 96 bottom, 100 bottom, 102 bottom, 103, 108, 110, 113 bottom, 122, 123, 124, 125 top, 126 & 127, 129, 130, 131, 132, 133, 134, 135, 136 bottom, 139, 145, 148, 150, 151 bottom, 152 & 153, 154 bottom, 155 top, 156, 157 bottom, 159, 160, 161 top, 162, 164 bottom, 170 middle, 171, 174, 175, 176, 177, 178-183.
Skandia Team GBR – Ocean Images: 10, 11, 26, 30, 34 & 35, 37, 41, 42, 68, 70 & 71, 78, 82 & 83, 86 bottom, 100 top, 102 top, 109 top, 113, 114 & 115, 118, 120 & 121, 136 top, 140 & 141, 142, 143, 146, 149, 151 top right, 155 middle and bottom, 158, 161 bottom, 166 & 167, 169 bottom, 170 bottom, 172 & 173, 174 bottom right, 184 & 185, 190.
RYA – Ocean Images: 23 top, 45 top, 52, 68 bottom, 90, 105, 109 bottom, 119, 137, 188 & 189.
RYA – Paul Wyeth: 25 top, 45, 48, 49, 96, 101, 104.
RS Racing – Paul Wyeth: front cover, 8, 9, 24, 29 top, 36, 38 & 39, 43, 53, 64, 69, 72 top, 74, 76, 79, 84, 93 bottom, 94 & 95, 97, 98, 106 & 107, 110, 111, 117, 125 bottom, 138, 144, 147, 151 top left, 154 top, 157 top, 166, 171 middle.
RS Racing – Mike Austen: 21 top right, 31 top, 77, 163, 164 top, 169 middle.
Volvo Champions Race: 40, 62 & 63, 72 bottom, 75, 88 & 89, 112, 116.
Minorca Sailing Holidays: 17 left, 18 left, 19 top left, 22 right, 65.
Adam May: 12 left. Tiggy Ansell: 58.

A CIP record of this book is available from the British Library.
Ring 0845 345 0400 for a free copy of our Publications Catalogue.

Totally Chlorine Free Sustainable Forests EMAS VERIFIED ENVIRONMENTAL MANAGEMENT

Published by **The Royal Yachting Association**
RYA House, Ensign Way, Hamble, Southampton SO31 4YA
Tel: 0845 345 0400
Fax: 0845 345 0329
Email: publications@rya.org.uk
Web: www.rya.org.uk

Note: While all reasonable care has been taken in the preparation of this book, the publisher takes no responsibility for the use of the methods or products or contracts described in the book.

Cover design: Pete Galvin.
Typeset: Jude Williams
Proof-reading and indexing: Alan Thatcher
Printed by: Printed in China through World Print

Contents

Contents

Contents

Foreword

It doesn't matter how placid you are in day to day life, deep down we all have a competitive streak lurking within us.

If you're a dinghy sailor, you may start off with every intention of just pottering around, but at some point you will feel the need to pit your wits against other sailors. The beauty is that there are plenty of worthy adversaries out there on the dinghy racing circuit.

I remember well my first time out racing in a dinghy and although I have raced many times since, I still recall how confusing things were on the start line. I also remember wishing that I had mugged up a bit on rules and technique prior to the race.

This is where Start to Race comes to the fore: It talks you through getting into racing in a logical, straightforward manner. There is a lot to learn when it comes to racing, but the beauty of this book is that at no point does that seem like a daunting task.

The book is also great if you have been out racing but are looking for ways to hone your skills and move up the fleet. There are plenty of very useful tips here that I wish I'd benefitted from when I was starting to race

I remain an avid fan of dinghy racing, I love the fact that it is not just a physical test, it is also about the mental battle and that, to me, is what sets it apart from many other sports.

This book helps unlock the door to new vistas of enjoyment out on the water and will help take your sailing on to another plane.

Happy racing!

Rod Carr OBE

1 | Why Race a Dinghy?

Dinghy racing is a superb sport which takes place in a thrilling environment, taking up the challenge provided by wind and water, stretching your physical and mental ability at all levels. Quite simply, there's no other sport like it...

Sail fast, have fun

Racing is the perfect way to enjoy dinghy sailing and improve your sailing skills at the same time. It is available at all levels from a fun race during a beach club holiday, to regular weekend or evening races at your local sailing club, to regional or national championships for the class of boat you choose to race, to European and World Championships staged by many different countries, to the Olympic sailing regatta which is staged every four years and is widely considered to be the pinnacle of dinghy racing pursued by an elite group of international sailors.

This book does not intend to provide tips and guidance for racing dinghies at the Olympics or any other top regatta dominated by professional teams. It is an introduction to racing from novice level, which will hopefully provide readers with enough confidence, knowledge and interest to have a go at dinghy racing, enjoy the experience and decide to keep racing with possible progress to bigger events and competition at a higher level.

Be warned that once you start, dinghy racing can become highly addictive. Many sailors are so hopelessly hooked that they dedicate a whole lifetime to racing. Children can take the tiller and start racing an Optimist from around five years of age; teenagers can move onto racing faster and flightier dinghies with spinnaker and trapeze; younger adults have a massive choice of dinghies that can be raced; older adults will probably start to move back into racing a dinghy that's predictable and stable, with the prospect of enjoying a competitive edge that will hopefully last to 80 years of age and beyond!

Virtually any type of dinghy can be raced. In this book we've listed some of the best-known international classes, but there are many different types available. Some sailors stay resolutely dedicated to a single class, while others chop and change as they progress through different aspects of the sport.

Five rewards are guaranteed, whatever dinghy you choose to race:

1. You will be pushed to improve boat-handling skills and consequently become a much better sailor, learning through practice and by following the example of better racers, as well as through your own mistakes.

2. You will exercise your brain, because dinghy racing is also a tactical sport that's not unlike a maritime form of chess in which natural elements hold the winning stake.

3. You will gain good friends on and off the water. Dinghy racing is a competitive sport, but amateur sailors should always expect to come ashore with a smile on their face and be ready to congratulate their opponents.

4. You will have the opportunity to travel and race in many different places. An added bonus is that dinghy racing is frequently staged in memorable sailing locations.

5. You will never get bored – the challenge is always there, at every level.

Enjoy the dinghy racing experience!

Where to next? Dinghy racing is a physical sport which also makes you think.

RS200s race on Lake Garda in northern Italy, a legendary location for superb wind.

2 | Racing Dinghy Classes

Any dinghy can be raced, either boat-for-boat or on handicap using the PY (Portsmouth Yardstick) rating scheme. There are a huge number of dinghy classes to choose from – here are some of the best known and most popular, with apologies to many other excellent classes that don't appear.

Olympic Classes

The selection of Olympic classes can be changed every four years. Most retain their position for a very long time.

Laser

The Laser is raced as an Olympic single-handed dinghy for men with the standard rig and Olympic single-handed dinghy for women with the smaller Radial rig. It's the world's biggest selling dinghy, with an absolute one-design format.

Crew:	One
Designer:	Bruce Kirby in 1971
Construction:	GRP
Hull:	59 kg
Length:	4.23 m
Beam:	1.42 m
Main:	Standard 7.06 sq m; Radial 5.7

Laser

Laser Radial

The Laser Radial is raced as the women's single-handed Olympic class and as an international youth class, with a smaller radial cut sail.

Crew:	One
Designer:	Bruce Kirby in 1971
Construction:	GRP
Hull:	59 kg
Length:	4.23 m
Beam:	1.42 m
Main:	Standard 5.7 sq m; Radial 5.7

Laser Radial

Finn

The heavyweight men's Olympic single-hander has been developed for modern racing with a sophisticated rig using a carbon mast and laminate sail.

Crew:	One
Designer:	Richard Sarby in 1949
Construction:	GRP foam sandwich
Hull:	120 kg
Length:	4.5 m
Beam:	1.5 m
Main:	10 sq m

Finn

470

The 470 was one of the first dinghies designed for glassfibre construction. It is raced as a men's and women's double-handed Olympic class with conventional symmetrical spinnaker.

Crew:	Two
Designer:	Andre Cornu in 1963
Construction:	GRP
Hull:	120 kg
Length:	4.7 m
Beam:	1.68 m
Main:	9.12 sq m
Jib:	3.58 sq m
Spinnaker:	14.3 sq m

49er

470

49er

Top performance skiff which was first raced at the Olympics in 2000. A bigger rig was introduced after the 2008 Olympics, to keep pace the development of crew skills.

Crew:	Two
Designer:	Julian Bethwaite in 1995
Construction:	GRP foam sandwich
Hull:	94 kg
Length:	4.99 m
Beam:	2.9 m
Main & Jib:	21.2 sq m
Asymmetric Spinnaker:	38 sq m

Classic Racing Classes

A small selection of leading classes that have stood the test of time for more than 40 years.

International 14

Twin trapeze development class allowing different 14 foot hull designs, rig variations and unlimited size spinnakers.

Crew:	Two
Designer:	Various since 1913
Construction:	GRP foam sandwich
Hull:	74.25 kg
Length:	4.27 m
Beam:	1.83 m
Main:	12.5 sq m
Jib:	5.6 sq m
Spinnaker:	unlimited size

International 14

International Moth

Single-handed development class which has adopted hydrofoils, boosting potential speed to over 20 knots. All up weight is around 28 kg. Recommended for 60-80 kg sailors with excellent reactions and balance!

Crew:	One
Designer:	Len Morris in 1928
Construction:	Carbon foam sandwich
Hull:	8 kg
Length:	3.35 m
Beam:	2.25 m
Main:	8 sq m

International Moth

Firefly

Originally raced as a single-handed Olympic class in 1948. The Firefly is popular as a team racing dinghy, due to its simple concept and excellent manoeuvrability.

Crew:	Two
Designer:	Uffa Fox in 1946
Construction:	Glassfibre or wood
Hull:	74 kg
Length:	3.65 m
Beam:	1.4 m
Main:	8.36 sq m
Jib:	2.52 sq m

Firefly

Merlin Rocket

A superb development class with a highly refined rig. No two designs are quite the same, so exclusivity is guaranteed.

Crew:	Two
Designer:	Various since 1946
Construction:	Wood or GRP foam sandwich
Hull:	98 kg
Length:	4.27 m
Beam:	2.2 m maximum
Main & Jib:	9.96 sq m
Spinnaker:	10 sq m

Merlin Rocket

International Canoe

One of the most challenging dinghies to sail, due to its super-narrow beam. The classic 2-sail version is lightning fast upwind, while the unlimited kite challenge is available to boost adrenaline offwind.

Crew:	One
Designer:	Various
Hull:	50 kg
Length:	5.18 m
Beam:	1.01 m
Main & Jib: up to 10 sq m	
Optional asymmetric spinnaker: unlimited area	

International canoe

GP14

Another popular classic design by Jack Holt, which is not only stable and easy to handle, but also provides competitive racing.

Crew:	Two
Designer:	Jack Holt in 1949
Construction:	Marine ply or GRP foam sandwich
Hull:	133 kg
Length:	4.27 m
Beam:	1.54 m
Main & Jib: 12.85 sq m	
Spinnaker: 8.4 sq m	

GP14

Enterprise

Classic double-handed dinghy with instantly recognisable blue mainsail and jib. After 50 years the class continues to provide excellent tactical racing and is particularly popular inland.

Crew:	Two
Designer:	Jack Holt in 1956
Construction:	Marine plywood or GRP foam sandwich
Hull:	94 kg
Length:	4.04 m
Beam:	1.6 m
Main & Jib:	10.7 sq m

Enterprise

Solo

One of Jack Holt's most popular designs, recommended for a crew weight from 65-100kg. Widely raced at inland and coastal locations, with one of the biggest championship turn-outs.

Crew:	One
Designer:	Jack Holt in 1956
Construction:	Marine plywood or GRP foam sandwich
Hull:	70 kg
Length:	3.78 m
Beam:	1.55 m
Main:	8.36 m

Solo

OK

OK

Classic single-hander with unstayed una-rig similar to a Finn. Has kept pace with modern developments by changing to a carbon mast.

Crew:	One
Designer:	Knud Olsen in 1957
Construction:	GRP foam sandwich
Hull:	72 kg
Length:	4 m
Beam:	1.2 m
Main:	9.45 sq m

Wayfarer

Wayfarer

Much loved cruiser-racer. The Mk4 version has a new cockpit layout designed by Phil Morrison and launched in 2007, but older boats remain equally competitive.

Crew:	Two
Designer:	Ian Proctor in 1957
Construction:	Marine plywood, glassfibre or foam sandwich
Hull:	168.7 kg
Length:	4.82 m
Beam:	1.86 m
Main:	8.83 sq m
Jib:	2.79 sq m
Spinnaker:	13.5 sq m

Europe

Former women's Olympic single-hander with advanced construction for hull and rig, best suited to lightweight racers.

Crew:	One
Designer:	Alois Roland in 1960
Construction:	GRP foam sandwich
Hull:	45 kg
Length:	3.35 m
Beam:	1.38 m
Main:	7 sq m

Europe

Scorpion

Unusual dinghy design which has been developed with a sophisticated and highly tweakable rig. Unlike most classes, wooden boats remain very popular.

Crew:	Two
Designer:	Taprell Dorling in 1960
Construction:	Wood or foam sandwich
Hull:	81 kg
Length:	4.27 m
Beam:	1.45 m
Main:	6.7 sq m
Jib:	3.25 sq m
Spinnaker:	11.14 sq m

Scorpion

Fireball

Fireball

Early skiff-style design which was far ahead of its time with single trapeze and spinnaker. Provides great racing in stronger winds.

Crew:	Two
Designer:	Peter Milne in 1962
Construction:	Epoxy foam sandwich
Hull:	79.4 kg
Length:	4.94 m
Beam:	1.37 m
Main & Jib:	11.43 sq m
Spinnaker:	13.01 sq m

505

505

Superb high performance dinghy with international racing circuit. Modern 505s have a highly adjustable rig for all wind conditions, combined with sophisticated hull and deck construction.

Crew:	Two
Designer:	John Westell in 1954
Construction:	Foam sandwich with carbon reinforcement or full carbon.
Hull:	127.4 kg minimum with fittings
Length:	5.05 m
Beam:	1.88 m
Main:	12.3 sq m
Jib:	4.94 sq m
Spinnaker:	27 sq m maximum

Contender

Trapeze single-hander with una-rig. Originally designed as a new Olympic class, but never selected.

Crew: One

Designer: Bob Miller in 1967

Construction: Wood or GRP foam sandwich

Hull: 83 kg

Length: 4.87 m

Beam: 1.5 m

Main: 10.8 sq m

Contender

Phantom

The Phantom has been brought up to date with superlight construction and a sophisticated rig with carbon spars. A top choice for heavier weight single-handed sailors.

Crew: One

Designer: Paul Wright and Brian Taylor in 1971

Construction: Epoxy foam sandwich

Hull: 61 kg

Length: 4.42 m

Beam: 1.64 m

Main: 9.75 sq m

Phantom

Streaker

Jack Holt's last major dinghy design has enjoyed a resurgence of popularity with new deck layout. Extremely simple and lightweight, with a wide competitive crew weight range from approximately 60-100kg.

Crew: One

Designer: Jack Holt in 1975

Construction: GRP foam sandwich

Hull: 48 kg

Length: 3.88 m

Beam: 1.37 m

Main: 6.5 sq m

Streaker

New Generation Classes

Asymmetric and skiff-style dinghy designs which race downwind from reach to reach. This style of racing kicked off in the 1990s.

B14

High power to weight ratio with huge asymmetric spinnaker probably makes the B14 the fastest non-trapeze double-hander in the world. Racks provide extra leverage for hiking.

Crew:	Two
Designer:	Julian Bethwaite in 1984
Construction:	GRP foam sandwich
Hull:	62 kg
Length:	4.5 m
Beam:	3.05 m
Main:	12 sq m
Jib:	5.2 sq m
Asymmetric Spinnaker:	29.2 sq m

B14

RS400

RS400

The first of the RS series of racing dinghy designs is rated as the classic hiking asymmetric for heavier weight crews.

Crew:	Two
Designer:	Phil Morrison in 1993
Construction:	GRP foam sandwich
Hull:	85 kg
Length:	4.52 m
Beam:	2 m
Main & Jib:	14.76 sq m
Asymmetric Spinnaker:	13.94 sq m

RS200

One of the most popular dinghy classes. The RS200 is a fast and highly manoeuvrable one-design which provides great racing for double-handed teams.

Crew:	Two
Designer:	Phil Morrison in 1995
Construction:	GRP foam sandwich
Hull:	78 kg
Length:	4 m
Beam:	1.83 m
Main & Jib:	11.52 sq m
Asymmetric Spinnaker:	8.29 sq m

RS200

Laser 2000

A stable and easily handled training boat with asymmetric spinnaker, which is also a popular choice for club racing.

Crew:	Two
Designer:	Phil Morrison in 1998
Construction:	GRP foam sandwich
Hull:	100 kg
Length:	4.44 m
Beam:	1.85 m
Main & Jib:	11.78 sq m
Asymmetric Spinnaker:	9.86 sq m

Laser 2000

Musto Skiff

Single-hander with racks, trapeze and asymmetric spinnaker. Awesome performance but you need to be fit!

Crew:	One
Designer:	Joachim Harpprecht in 1999
Construction:	Carbon glass foam sandwich
Hull:	43 kg
Length:	4.55 m
Beam:	2.3 m
Main:	11.8 sq m
Asymmetric Spinnaker:	15.5 sq m

Musto Skiff

RS800

A twin wire skiff with racks, performance equalisation to even out crews with different weights and heights, plus an asymmetric spinnaker. This class brings high performance sailing within reach of most good sailors.

Crew:	Two
Designer:	Phil Morrison in 1999
Construction:	GRP foam sandwich
Hull:	62 kg
Length:	4.8 m
Beam:	1.88-2.89 m with adjustable racks
Main & Jib:	16.5 sq m
Asymmetric Spinnaker:	21 sq m

RS800

RS700

RS500

Single trapeze, double-handed dinghy with oversize asymmetric spinnaker to boost performance. Great fun for lighter weight crews.

Crew:	Two
Designer:	Phil Morrison in 2006
Construction:	GRP foam sandwich
Hull:	77 kg
Length:	4.34 m
Beam:	1.58 m
Main & Jib:	9.5 sq m
Asymmetric Spinnaker:	14 sq m

RS700

Single-handed skiff with trapeze and spinnaker. Direct competitor to the Musto Skiff.

Crew:	One
Designer:	Nick Peters & Alex Newton in 2000
Construction:	GRP foam sandwich
Hull:	56 kg
Length:	4.68 m
Beam:	1.92-2.33 m with adjustable racks
Main:	12.8 sq m
Asymmetric Spinnaker:	16 sq m

RS500

Topper Xenon

Modern rotomoulded dinghy which has been used for the Endeavour Trophy, an annual 'champion of champions' event for all dinghy classes.

Crew:	Two
Designer:	Ian Howlett in 2005
Construction:	Rotomoulded polyethylene
Length:	4.5 m
Beam:	2 m
Main & Jib:	15.5 sq m
Asymmetric Spinnaker:	12.75 sq m

Junior Classes

Recommended for a maximum age of 15-16 years, as a pathway to youth classes.

Cadet

Laser 4.7

Virtually the same as the standard Laser single-hander with a smaller 4.7 rig recommended for maximum age 15-16.

Crew:	One
Designer:	Bruce Kirby in 1971
Construction:	GRP
Hull:	59 kg
Length:	4.23 m
Beam:	1.42 m
Main:	4.7 sq m

Cadet

Classic pram bow international double-handed racing class with symmetric spinnaker.

Crew:	Two
Designer:	Jack Holt in 1947
Construction:	Marine plywood, GRP or GRP foam sandwich
Hull:	54 kg
Length:	3.22 m
Beam:	1.27 m
Main:	3.9 sq m
Jib:	1.26 sq m
Spinnaker:	4.25 sq m

Laser 4.7

Mirror

Jack Holt's last design is established as a popular choice for double-handed junior racing. The latest Mirrors can race with an optional bermudan rig or newly designed cockpit layout.

Crew:	Two
Designer:	Jack Holt in 1963
Construction:	Marine ply or GRP foam sandwich
Hull:	45 kg
Length:	3.33 m
Beam:	1.4 m
Main:	3.6 sq m
Jib:	3.6 sq m
Spinnaker:	6.5 sq m

Mirror

Optimist

Exceptionally popular and competitive international single-handed racing class powered by a distinctive lateen rig. The Optimist can be carried on a car roof rack, allowing parents to easily drive children to events!

Crew: One

Designer: Clark Mills in 1947

Construction: Marine ply, GRP or GRP foam sandwich

Hull: 35 kg

Length: 2.3 m

Beam: 1.13 m

Main: 3.59 sq m

Optimist

RS Tera

Small, low cost single-hander which has built rapid support as a junior racing class.

Crew: One

Designer: Paul Handley in 2005

Construction: Rotomoulded polyethylene

Hull: 35 kg

Length: 2.87 m

Beam: 1.23 m

Main: 4.8 sq m

RS Tera

RS Feva

RS Feva

One-design junior international racing class with asymmetric spinnaker. The Feva has a rotomoulded hull for durability and low price, and is also an excellent choice for learning to handle a small performance boat.

Crew: Two

Designer: Paul Handley in 2002

Construction: Polyethylene

Hull: 63 kg

Length: 3.64 m

Beam: 1.42 m

Main: 6.5 sq m

Jib: 2.1 sq m

Spinnaker: 7 sq m

Topper

Topper

Very simple and very popular single-handed racing class for junior sailors in the UK. 'Topper' refers to its 'car toppability'.

Crew: One

Designer: Ian Proctor in 1976

Construction: Polyethylene

Hull: 43 kg

Length: 3.4 m

Beam: 1.2 m

Main: 5.2 sq m

Youth Classes

Recommended for under 19 year old sailors who can race in the ISAF Youth World Championships.

Laser Radial

Laser Radial

Virtually the same as the standard Laser single-hander with mid-size Radial rig, recommended for girls and boys in the 60-70kg weight range. The Laser Radial is an Olympic and ISAF Youth World Championship class for women.

Crew:	One
Designer:	Bruce Kirby in 1971
Construction:	GRP
Hull:	59 kg
Length:	4.23 m
Beam:	1.42 m
Main:	5.7 sq m

Laser

The Laser is an Olympic and ISAF Youth World Championship class for men, recommended for the 72-83kg weight range. It is also the world's best selling sailboat – a total one-design with a simple, unstayed rig.

Crew:	One
Designer:	Bruce Kirby in 1971
Construction:	GRP
Hull:	59 kg
Length:	4.23 m
Beam:	1.42 m
Main:	7.06 sq m

Laser

420

One of the first dinghies to be designed for glassfibre construction, fitted with symmetrical spinnaker and single trapeze. The 420 is a true international class which is raced at ISAF Youth World Championship events.

Crew:	Two
Designer:	Christian Maury in 1960
Construction:	GRP
Hull:	80 kg
Length:	4.2 m
Beam:	1.63 m
Main:	10.25 sq m
Jib:	2.8 sq m
Spinnaker:	9 sq m

420

29er racing at RYA Youth National Championship.

29er

The scaled-down 49er provides a skiff option to the 420 at ISAF Youth World Championship events.

Crew:	Two
Designer:	Julian Bethwaite in 1997
Construction:	Glassfibre foam sandwich
Hull:	70 kg
Length:	4.4 m
Beam:	1.7 m
Main & Jib:	12 sq m
Asymmetric Spinnaker:	16 sq m

Youth and Junior Racing

The RYA Youth and Junior Racing programmes provide an incredible opportunity for young sailors to improve their sailing skills, discover racing and progress to higher goals. The annual Zone and Home Country Championships attract more than a thousand boats, while the RYA supports more than five hundred of the more seasoned sailors at over fifty international regattas each season, including major events such as the Youth Sailing ISAF World Championships. The programmes provide progression through a series of squads, from zone to national level, with the finest and most committed sailors eventually progressing to Olympic level. It also provides a clear development pathway through RYA recognised junior and youth classes towards the Olympic classes. The programme is backed up by the Volvo RYA Champion Club Scheme, ensuring coaching and support at local level.

www.rya.org.uk

3 | Choosing a Racing Dinghy

If you want to race a dinghy, there is a huge choice. Where do you start looking, where should you race and what type of boat will suit you best?

Popularity

Some racing dinghy classes are much more popular than others. In terms of numbers the Laser is the runaway winner because it first appeared at just the right time, is reasonably cheap to buy, is neither expensive nor time consuming to own, is great fun to race for a wide range of abilities and has remained a fairly timeless design. At the other end of the scale, a dinghy like the International Canoe is highly specialised, extremely expensive and very difficult to control, providing the ultimate dinghy racing challenge for a small group of enthusiasts.

A good clue to popularity is provided by national championship attendance. During 2007, five classes had 100+ entries at their week-long national championship:

Optimist	379 entries
Topper	289 entries
Cadet	162 entries
Laser Radial	142 entries
RS200	126 entries

Other top classes with national championship entries of more than 50 included the Solo, Laser (standard), Merlin Rocket, 420, Mirror, Phantom, Pico, RS Feva, Salcombe Yawl, RS400, Lark, Enterprise, Scorpion, Firefly, 29er, Streaker, International 14, RS700, Laser 4.7, RS800 and Contender.

Classes, which have a large national championship entry, will generally have well attended racing at other national and possibly international regattas. Most classes run a 'travellers series' of a dozen or more weekend events throughout the main sailing season, plus other delights such as inland and end of season championships. All details should be shown on the class website, which invariably provides a mine of information as enthusiastic members attempt to 'sell' their class to other sailors.

RS Fevas provide double-handed junior crews with exciting racing.

RS200 – top choice for adults who want a hiking asymmetric dinghy.

The Topper is established as a favourite junior class.

Location

For many people, it makes sense to belong to a sailing club, which has specific advantages:

- Convenient to travel to with easy launching and a great sailing location.

- Supports a class you would like to sail. This includes organising regular racing at weekends and on summer evenings, as well as possible winter series and expert training days.

- Good boat park and club changing or catering facilities which will help make your dinghy racing as hassle free as possible.

- Friendly members, both round the race course and on shore.

- Guaranteed safety cover while you are racing.

Cadets racing inland on a tight reach at RYA Eric Twiname Championships.

The unusual grass roofed sailing club at Malcesine on Lake Garda provides a superb venue for championship events.

Inland or Coastal?

Whether you choose to race at an inland or coastal club may be decided by location. There may be other specific advantages and disadvantages.

Coastal Plus

It's great to race on the open sea which provides plenty of space and the opportunity for sailing in waves. Unless the wind is offshore, it should be steady. In warm weather, dinghy racers can reap the benefits of a sea breeze. Coastal clubs are often perfect for asymmetric and skiff style racing which requires a lot of fast reaching offwind.

Coastal Minus

It can get so windy that racing is blown out, with waves making conditions unforgiving. Tides may mean there is no water – some clubs can only race every other week. Seawater is sticky, salty and corrosive each time you race.

Inland Plus

Racing will generally be possible, whatever the wind. If things go wrong, it's not far back to the shore. Great for short course tactical racing, with a lot of tacking on wind shifts. Racing on fresh water is more pleasant for your body and your boat!

Inland Minus

Wind may be very gusty, variable or light, particularly if it has to blow over hills, houses and trees. Limited sailing area may be unsuitable for racing an asymmetric class. No waves to add interest to your racing.

Lots of wind shifts can be expected on a lake surrounded by trees.

The joy of blasting across waves on the open water of a coastal course. Hannah Mills and Katrina Hughes in action at Weymouth.

Resale

The overall cost of owning a racing dinghy will be governed by its resale value. There is a guaranteed market for popular one-design racing classes, which makes them easier to buy or sell second-hand. This is particularly true if the boat is maintained in top condition.

This Cadet is guaranteed to provide total satisfaction in such great condition. Wooden boats race on equal terms with glassfibre.

Upkeep and Time

A small, simple, one-design class like the Laser or Topper is inexpensive to own with the cheapest slots in the dinghy park and little upkeep required. Replacement of new parts should be kept to a minimum, although it's worth mentioning that Olympic Laser sailors tend to buy a new sail for every major event – such expense is not normal for club racers! More complex, high performance boats tend to be more expensive and time consuming to own. The boat will need to be carefully maintained. Control lines and shock cords will need replacing. Daggerboard and rudder blades will be vulnerable to 'dings' which must be repaired. Rigging up or packing up will take a longer time.

You not only have to look after the hull and deck – control lines, elastics and toestraps must be maintained.

One-design or development class?

- Most modern racing dinghy classes are one-designs. All boats have the same hull shape, rig and fittings, so it is purely the ability of the crew which decides the race.

- Most of the older classic classes are virtual one-designs, but there may be a choice of different boat builders and sailmakers servicing the class, with different hull materials such as wood or foam sandwich and different control systems for the rig. There may also be tolerances in the shape of the hull, which were originally allowed for marine plywood construction. Surprisingly, this makes little difference to relative boat speed.

- Development classes range from 'restricted development in which a class keeps a tight rein on the rules, to unrestricted development in which anything goes within a few simple parameters. Cost and complexity will tend to increase as restrictions are lifted, encouraging endless new designs and exotic materials.

The National 12 is a classic development class, open to different designs.

Classic or Modern?

- Classic dinghies are perfectly suited to racing upwind, on a reach and dead downwind with or without a symmetrical spinnaker. Racing can be enjoyed in almost all conditions, including light winds.

- Modern dinghies fitted with asymmetric spinnakers are perfectly suited to racing upwind and on a reach, but close to hopeless for racing directly downwind when they lose all speed. They sail much faster by gybing downwind on a series of broad reaches, following a zig-zag course from gybe to gybe. This requires a lot of space on the water and relies on high VMG (velocity made good) to race to the leeward mark in the shortest possible time. Asymmetric racing is best in a moderate or fresh breeze, and is not so great in light winds when it is difficult to make up downwind VMG.

A 30-year old Lark still provides great racing.

Single-handed or Double-handed?

Racing single-handed:

• You are never stuck because you can't find a crew.

• If things go wrong in the race, there is only yourself to blame.

• Single-handed dinghies are generally cheaper and simpler to own.

• Some of the most popular dinghy classes are single-handers including the Laser, Optimist, Topper and Solo.

Racing double-handed:

• Top choice if you want to race with a favourite person – girlfriend, boyfriend, wife, husband, son, daughter, best pal.

• It's nice to have someone to bounce ideas off, discuss tactics, help rig, launch and pack up the boat, and talk about the racing when it's all over.

• Racing with a spinnaker generally (but not always) requires two crew. The spinnaker can add a lot of fun and interest to your racing.

• Racing with a trapeze generally (but not always) requires two crew, also adding a lot of fun and interest to your racing.

"I want to talk during the race." Then you should race a double-hander.

"I want to be alone." Then you should race a single-hander. The 4.7 is recommended for junior sailors up to 16.

Height and Weight

All dinghies are weight sensitive and have an optimum weight range for best racing performance. If you are too heavy, the boat will drag through the water and slow down. If you are too light, you will have insufficient weight to sail the boat at full power in stronger winds.

Most dinghy classes publish a recommended weight range for the crew. For instance:

Finn	80-110kg
49er	148-160kg
International Moth	60-80kg
Laser	65-85kg
Laser 2000	120-180kg
Merlin Rocket	140-170kg
Mirror	80-100kg
Optimist	40-45kg
RS200	115-145kg
RS700	66-100kg
RS800	127-160kg
RS Feva	80-115kg
Solo	65-100kg
29er	105-140kg

You need to eat plenty of pies to sail a Finn!

- Height may also play an important role on a trapeze boat. In simple terms, a tall thin sailor who weighs 70kg will have more leverage than a short fat sailor who weighs 70kg!

- Some classes 'equalise' weight by weighing the crew and adding an appropriate amount of extra lead weight to the boat. Height can also be 'equalised' by using adjustable width racks.

Technical and Physical Ability

Many racing dinghies are fairly easy boats to handle if you have moderate sailing ability. Nor do they require a particularly high level of physical fitness to compete in races at local or national level.

Some racing dinghies are very demanding in terms of boat handling, fitness and agility – for instance, racing a Musto Skiff or 49er will make extreme demands on the crew.

You need to be agile and fit to sail a 49er! Ian Martin and Ben McGrane storm away from the start line.

Aspirations

Where do you want to go with your racing? Junior and Youth sailors have an established pathway which supports specific single-handed and double-handed classes. This is designed to prepare the elite for Olympic sailing competition. But the vast majority of dinghy racers of all ages have no Olympic aspirations. For them, it is a fantastic choice with every conceivable style of dinghy racing available.

The Feva shown here provides a great low cost introduction to racing with an asymmetric spinnaker. It provides a direct link to mastering faster and more challenging boats like the RS200, which can in turn lead to trapezing single-handed on the RS700 or double-handed on the RS800.

Racing downwind with a pack of RS Fevas following close behind.

National Sailing Academy

The Weymouth & Portland National Sailing Academy (WPNSA) is a **super club**, which will host the sailing event in the 2012 Olympics. This superb facility was formed as a not for profit company which officially opened on 1st April 2000. The academy exists to promote the sport of sailing at all levels of competence and ability, through courses, training and events to include all people, especially those with difficulties. It also exists to provide a facility for the community, for example actively encouraging Dorset schools to bring sailing into their outdoor activities. Annual and day membership is available, together with extensive storage for dinghies which can be launched directly onto the superb sailing ground provided by Portland Harbour. The WPNSA is a favourite location for class training, with regattas and championships staged throughout the main season.

www.wpnsa.org.uk

4 | RYA Portsmouth Yardstick Scheme

How do you race with different classes of dinghy? The RYA Portsmouth Yardstick is a handicap system designed to provide a 'corrected time' for all finishers…

The RYA Portsmouth Yardstick scheme is a method of applying handicaps to allow different dinghy classes as well as cruising yachts to compete in the same race. It is based on race results sent in by sailing clubs at the end of each year, from which Portsmouth Numbers (PN) are allocated to new classes or updated for existing classes. Each type of boat is allocated a PN ranging from 1400 through to 820 depending on its performance.

The lower the number, the faster the boat. If a boat with a PN of 950 takes 950 seconds to race round a course, a boat with a number of 1050 should cover the same course in 1050 seconds to be equal on corrected time.

Origins of the PY Scheme

The RYA originally launched the RYA Portsmouth Yardstick Scheme for dinghies and keelboats in 1952, allowing different boats to compete on equal terms. Allocating numbers has become a lot more complex in recent years, due to some dinghy classes being raced in a variety of modes – for instance with different rigs, with and without spinnakers, single-handed or with two crew. Three years of return data are now required for PN assessment, ensuring that different modes of dinghy can be identified more clearly.

RS200, Blaze and Lark battle for position while rounding a mark during the annual Frensham Frenzy pursuit race, with an Illusion 2.4 metre keelboat beating up to the mark in the background. All these different classes can race together, thanks to the Portsmouth Yardstick Scheme.

Definitions

- Portsmouth Numbers (PN) are measures of performance, representing times over a common but unspecified distance.
- Primary Yardsticks (PY) are Portsmouth Numbers published by the RYA and well attested by clubs over several years.
- Secondary Yardsticks (SY) are Portsmouth Numbers published by the RYA, but not as consistently attested as PY numbers.
- Recorded Numbers (RN) are Portsmouth Numbers published by the RYA on the basis of limited information.
- Club Numbers (CN) are Portsmouth Numbers allocated by clubs. They can be derived from Trial Numbers or adjusted from RYA lists.
- Trial Numbers (TN) are Portsmouth Numbers allocated by a club and the RYA until a CN is assessed and allocated.

Calculating corrected time

Every boat must be timed when it crosses the finish line. Corrected time is calculated using the following formula:

Corrected Time (C) = Elapsed Time (E) divided by Portsmouth Number (PN) x 1000.

Pursuit Racing

The hare and tortoise style of pursuit racing provides an enjoyable alternative with one big advantage – the boat which is leading at the end of the race is the winner, since all the time calculations have been done before the start of the race.

- Starting times are calculated for a specific race duration (RD) that will suit the spread of different boats taking part in the race. If 90 minutes is chosen as the RD related to boat X with a PN of 1200, then the expected RD for boat Y with a PN of 1000 would be 75 minutes and for boat Z with a PN of 1400 it would be 105 minutes. These times are simple ratios – 1200/90 = 1000/75 = 1400/105.
- Start time for boat Y would be 75-90 = 15 minutes after boat X. Start time for boat Z would be 105-90 = 15 minutes before boat X.
- The start boat may show large numerical cards to indicate the number of minutes that have elapsed since the first start, with sound signals for each subsequent start.
- The finish needs to be as close to the end of the RD as possible.

Topper Xenon races against RS Vision. The Vision is badly placed in the Xenon's dirty wind and should tack to get clear air.

5 Race as Helm or Crew?

Some people want to race as helm, others prefer to race as crew, but the skills required are very similar and will contribute to a winning team. Never assume that the crew is someone who just provides ballast to hold up the boat!

"What, me worried?" If you're the perfect team, the crew will have total faith in the helm and the helm will have total faith in the crew. Nick Rogers and Joe Glanfield race in strong winds at Hyères.

5 | Race as Helm or Crew?

Crewing provides a great introduction to racing, without the commitment to buy your own boat. But it is important to find a good helm who will provide a positive experience from which you can learn about racing. So when possible, aim to crew for a helm who has the potential to win.

Traditionally, the helm is regarded as the skipper of the boat who has the ultimate choice which way to turn. However, this cannot work if helm and crew don't work as a team. In some situations, the helm will rely on the crew to ease or pull the sheet to allow the boat to bear away or head up, which relies on both crew working in perfect harmony.

Many of the classic dinghy classes rely heavily on the skills of the helm – a good crew may not be able to win races with an average helm, but a good helm may be able to win races with an average crew. If the boat has a spinnaker, the input of the crew greatly increases. If the boat is a lightweight, high performance flyer with a huge asymmetric spinnaker and trapezes, helm and crew are likely to play an equal role in maximising performance round the track.

You may hear a helm shouting at the crew, or maybe the crew shouting back. Never do that! Respect your crew (or helm) at all times and learn how to get over disagreements fast. Move forward by discussing what went wrong; or better still what went right with the race! Always remember that racing is a sport which the great majority of people quite rightly regard as pure fun.

Size and Shape

If you are very serious about racing, the choice of being helm or crew may be decided by your physique. For instance, if a double-handed class has a single trapeze, optimum performance will normally be obtained with a crew who is heavier or taller than the helm, providing maximum leverage to hold the boat upright with the trapeze. The optimum weight for a 470 is reckoned to be about 60kg for the helm and 70kg for the crew. If a double-handed class provides helm and crew with equal leverage, either by both crew hiking on a class such as the RS200 or both crew twin-trapezing on a class such as the RS800, weight and height can be closely matched. However, many classes are designed to favour a heavier helmsman who can provide most leverage in the widest part of the boat, as well as keeping crew weight centred which will help to reduce pitching.

The crew has three primary tasks upwind – trimming the jib, hiking out and looking ahead.

Sailing as a team

Helm and crew should aim to sail as a team who provide equal input towards racing the boat. Your idea of success may mean being a winner, or simply ensuring that every race is an enjoyable experience. Whatever your aspirations, it is crucial that the helm has faith in the crew and vice versa. This faith may be based on personal friendship or sailing ability, depending on how serious you are about the sport.

The perfect helm and crew will develop an empathy that allows them to function as a single unit. Everything necessary to make the boat go fast will be accomplished automatically, because both helm and crew know exactly what they are doing. The helm and crew will share the work required to go racing – for instance preparing and rigging the boat – but should also identify who is best suited to specific tasks, both on and off the water.

It is important to get experience at both ends of the boat. For instance, a crew who can also helm – often through single-handed racing experience – will have a much greater understanding of the helm's requirements and difficulties during a race. Plus, if the helm falls over the side and gets left behind, the crew can take control of the boat!

Top Tips for helms and crews

By Alan Olive, former Coaching Development Manager at the RYA.

- Crew and helm are equally important and their opinions are of equal value.

- Effective communication is the essence of teamwork.

- Focus on how to succeed, not on what went wrong. Mistakes are there to create action plans for how to get better.

- Use exercises such as eyes shut helming/crewing or mouth shut sailing to develop communication during races.

- Develop language that allows each sailor to vent any anger without upsetting the other. Humour is great for this. Do not accept bullying of any kind.

- Aim to resolve problems, not to blame the other person. Try to identify what is going wrong from each sailor's perspective, then work to overcome those problems.

A dynamic boat like the 49er simply won't 'go' if the helm and crew don't work together. It takes a lot of practice to get this right.

Close quarters racing during the RS Eurocup on Lake Garda.
It's vital to know who has right of way and who should give way.

Racing Rules | 6

Racing rules are based on rights of way. Sticking to the rules is vital to ensure fair competition, without collisions or danger round the course.

6 | Racing Rules

Getting started

The Racing Rules of Sailing (RRS) say which boat has right of way when two boats meet. The boat that does not have right of way must keep clear. This helps avoid collisions, which might not only damage the boat but injure the sailors as well. Sailors use the Racing Rules tactically, to get an advantage over other boats. The Racing Rules are updated every four years. They are available on the ISAF website (*www.sailing.org*) and are published by the RYA as the Racing Rules of Sailing 2009 – 2012, product code YR1. This 169-page book (printed on waterproof paper!) contains all the rules, as well as specialist appendices that are needed only occasionally or that apply only to special types of racing.

Who has right of way? It's the right-hand 49er, so the left-hand 49er which is overtaking on the windward side must point up and keep clear.

Principles

Fundamental principles include safety, fair sailing and acceptance of rules.

- Competitors should be provided with racing that is fair, enjoyable and safe.
- Always show courtesy and respect to other competitors and race officials, as well as to other people on the water. You must race fairly, comply with the rules and not bring the sport into disrepute.
- If you break a rule, you should promptly take a penalty. Sometimes the penalty is to do a single turn, sometimes it is two turns, and sometimes it is to retire and leave the race.
- During a race, you must be prepared to give all possible help to any person or boat in danger.
- It is for you alone to decide whether it is safe for you to start or continue racing, not for the people running the race.

Rights of Way

The basic right of way rules, which are used for all sailing, are paramount when racing:

RRS10. When boats meet on opposite tacks, port tack gives way.

A boat is on port or starboard tack when its port or starboard side is closer to the wind, making it the windward side. When running by the lee, the leeward side is the same side as the mainsail.

Orange must give way to green both upwind and downwind.

Port tack must give way if there is likely to be a contact, but 07 appears to have cleared the starboard tack boats.

RRS11. *When boats meet on the same tack and are overlapped, the windward boat must keep clear.*

Two boats on the same tack overlap when neither is clear astern, or when a boat between them overlaps both.

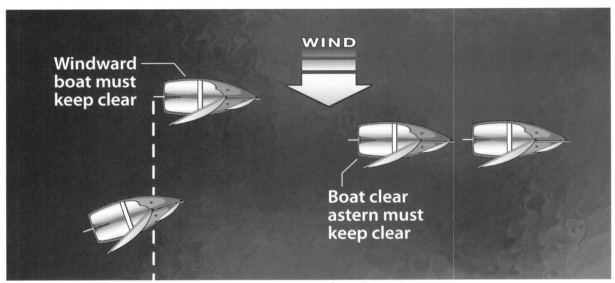

Orange and green are overlapped.   Orange is clear astern.

A tight situation. 066 has right of way over 024, but must give way to the leeward boat on the right side of the picture.

RRS12. *When boats meet on the same tacks and are not overlapped, the boat clear astern must keep clear of the boat that is clear ahead.*

When are you clear ahead or clear astern?

Clear astern: A boat is clear astern when her hull and equipment in normal position are behind a line abeam from the aftermost point of the other boat's hull and equipment (including the rudder) in normal position. The other boat is clear ahead.

Overlap: Boats overlap if neither is clear astern or when a boat between them overlaps both.

Clear ahead: A boat is clear ahead when her hull and equipment in normal position are ahead of a line abeam from the forward point of the other boat's hull and equipment (including the spinnaker) in normal position.

As the fleet approaches the leeward mark, 1147, overlapped to windward of the middle boat, must keep clear of the middle boat, while the middle boat overlapped to windward of 896 must keep clear of 896. There may be more overlaps as well!

Keep clear when tacking

RRS13. *After a boat passes head to wind, she shall keep clear of other boats until she is on a close-hauled course.*

The green boat is now on starboard tack, and the orange boat is on port tack. But because the green boat has passed head to wind, it is the green boat that must keep clear, until she is on a close-hauled course. It is only then that RRS10 starts to apply (see page 41), when the port-tack orange boat has to keep clear. But the green boat must tack far enough away to allow her to do so (see RRS15).

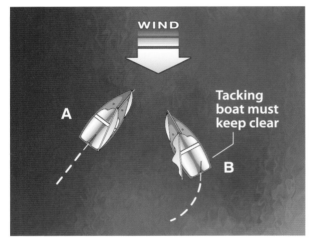

The green boat has passed head to wind, but is not yet close-hauled on the new starboard tack, so must keep clear, while tacking, of the orange boat.

Who has right of way? Don't be too aggressive with port tack boats – if you give them some space, they may return the favour at a later date.

If you don't get clear of the start, you will need to tack to clear your wind as soon as possible. GBR3 had to choose the right moment to tack across all the boats on starboard. It can be difficult to find enough space to complete your tack in a tight pack of boats.

Avoiding contact

RRS14. *A boat must avoid contact with another boat if reasonably possible.*

Even if a boat has right of way, she must try to avoid a collision.

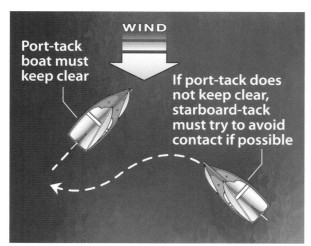

Even if you have right of way, you cannot ram a port tack boat. It is your responsibility to take avoiding action.

Lack of steerage in very light winds can cause problems with contact rules! You need eyes in the back of your head!

Acquiring right of way

RRS15. *When a boat acquires right of way, she must initially give the other boat room to keep clear (unless she has acquired right of way due to the other boat's actions).*

For instance, a boat which is attempting to overtake from clear astern must initially keep clear of the boat clear ahead. When the overtaking boat becomes overlapped to leeward, she now gains right of way under RRS11, but she must do so far enough away from the other boat that the other boat has room to keep clear if she 'moves over' immediately.

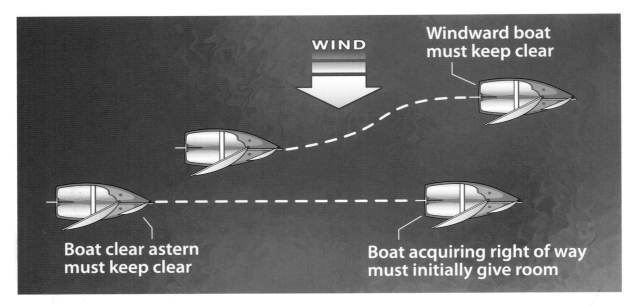

WIND

Windward boat must keep clear

Boat clear astern must keep clear

Boat acquiring right of way must initially give room

Changing course

RRS16. *When a right of way boat changes course, she must give the other boat room to keep clear.*

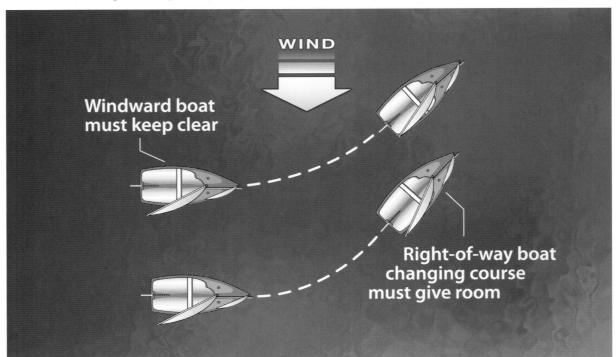

WIND

Windward boat must keep clear

Right-of-way boat changing course must give room

Proper course

RRS17. This rule applies when boats are within two lengths of each other. A boat that becomes overlapped to leeward from clear astern must not 'sail above' (luff to windward of) her proper course while the overlap exists.

A 'proper course' is the course a boat would sail to finish as soon as possible in the absence of the other boat. There is no proper course before the starting signal.

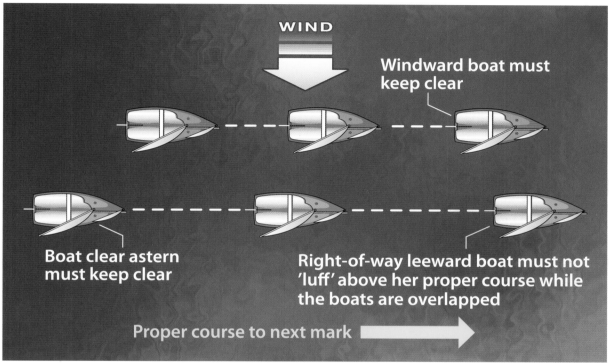

Holding a proper course may not be so easy, rolling downwind with overlaps to windward and leeward!

unding rules

Rules become more complex when boats meet at marks of the course where there is greatest potential for collision. If in doubt, best practice is to allow plenty of room and keep clear. Everyone would like to be the boat nearest the mark. RRS 10, 11, 12 and 13 are not enough on their own to make mark-rounding fair, and so RRS18 adds to some of those rules and sometimes relaxes them. Rule 19 deals with similar problems at an obstruction, which is an object that needs a big change of course to pass, for instance, a moored yacht.

Leading boats have a huge advantage, because they are clear of the crowd trying to squeeze round the mark. In this kind of situation, avoiding collisions and finding clean wind become critical.

RRS18. When boats are overlapped, the outside boat shall give the inside boat 'mark-room', which is room to sail to the mark, and then room to sail a proper course while at the markroom.

This may prevent a boat from taking advantage of her right of way. This is usually decided when the 'zone' is reached – the area that is within three hull-lengths of the mark – and if boats are overlapped there, one of them will be the inside boat. If they are not overlapped the one astern must give mark-room to the boat ahead.

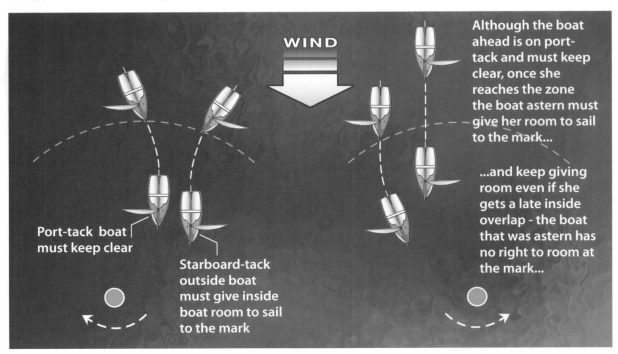

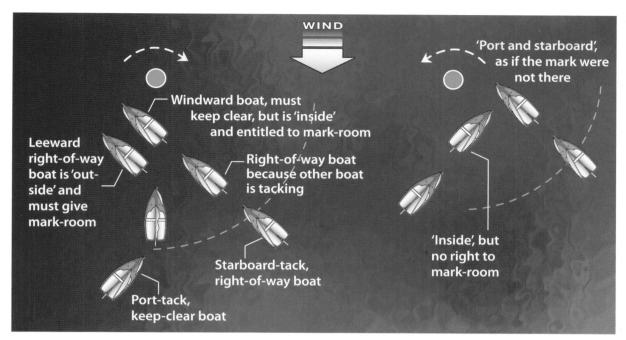

At windward marks, RRS applies only when boats are on the same tack. The 'zone' is irrelevant to boats that were not on the same tack before they entered it. Mark-room includes room for an inside boat to tack to round the mark.

At a windward mark, when boats that are overlapped on the same tack enter the zone, Rule 18.2(b) says that the outside boat must keep clear AND give room to the inside boat to round the mark. But when a boat is 'subject to Rule 13' (between head to wind and close-hauled') while in the 'zone' when another boat is able to round the mark without having to put in a tack, RRS 18.3 says that the boat that tacked into a right-of-way position inside the zone (clear ahead or overlapped to leeward) must not make the other boat sail above close-hauled (or bear away and miss out the mark) in order to keep clear.

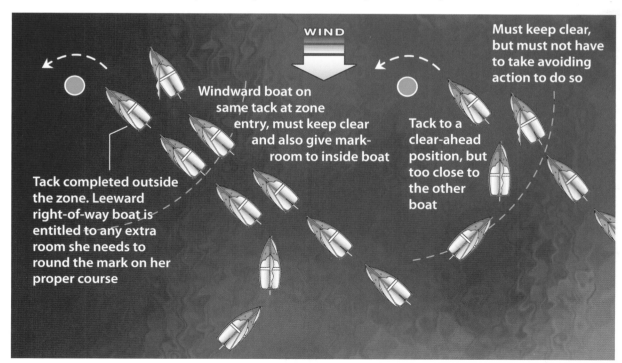

Room to tack at an obstruction

RRS20. When you are close-hauled and are unable to tack to avoid an obstruction, you may hail for room to tack.

This means you cannot be forced onto the rocks! Instead, call "Room to tack". Before tacking, you must give the hailed boat time to respond. The other boat should tack as soon as possible or alternatively call "You tack" and allow room. In both cases, you must also tack as soon as possible. This rule does not apply at a starting mark surrounded by navigable water, which is big enough to be an obstruction (like a committee boat), when boats are starting.

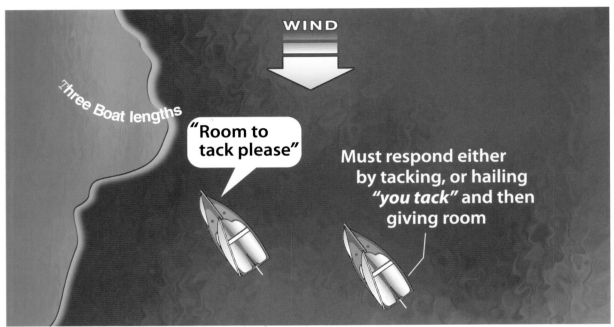

Leading boats have a huge advantage, because they are clear of the crowd trying to squeeze round the mark. In this kind of situation, avoiding collisions and finding clean wind become critical.

You can ask for "water!" to avoid hitting the land. It's just a matter of being sensible and remembering that dinghy racing is a sport!

Penalty turns

RRS44.1 When you touch a mark of the course, you may exonerate yourself by taking a One-Turn Penalty. When you break any of the rules 10 to 23 that apply 'when boats meet', you may exonerate yourself by taking a Two-Turns Penalty.

Both penalties must be taken well clear of other boats that are racing. If you take a penalty at the finishing line, you must sail completely to the course side of the line before finishing.

The One-Turn Penalty and Two-Turns Penalty are not available if you caused serious damage or injury, or if you gained a significant advantage when you broke the rule. Instead, you must retire.

- When making a penalty turn on the windward leg, you need to minimise being blown downwind. The gybe must be as fast as possible, while the tack is less critical.
- When making a penalty turn on the leeward leg, you need to minimise being blown upwind. The tack must be as fast as possible, while the gybe is less critical.

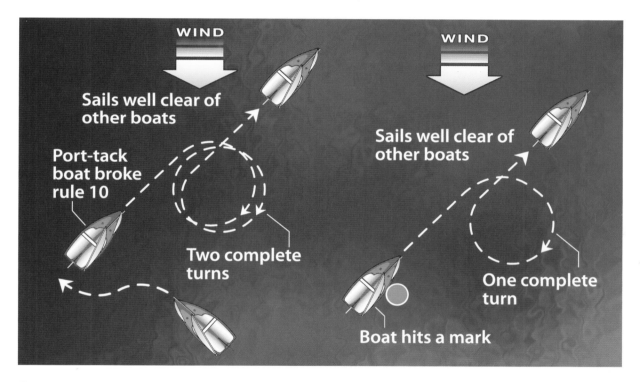

Propulsion

RRS42. With some exceptions, you must use only wind and water to increase, maintain or decrease boat speed. You may adjust the trim of sails and the hull, but must not move your body to propel the boat.

There are two principal exceptions. Firstly, you may move your body to roll the boat through a tack or gybe, provided that your boat speed immediately afterwards is not greater than it would have been without a tack or gybe. Secondly, the crew may pull the sheet of any sail (including the spinnaker guy) in order to start planing on a gust of wind or surfing on a wave, but only once for each gust or wave. This does not apply when beating to windward.

Protests and Redress

RRS60-62.

If you are involved in an incident and think the other boat has broken a rule, you may protest. You must inform the other boat by shouting "Protest!" You will also need to lodge the protest in writing, but do not need to go ahead with the protest if you change your mind.

If you believe your finishing position has been made significantly worse because the race committee has done something wrong, you may be able to get redress, often in the form of points, for an estimated finishing position. This may also apply if another breaks a rule, resulting in physical injury or damage to your boat. You need to apply in writing to the protest committee.

ISAF INTRODUCTORY RULES FOR RACING

Some competitors will seek to exploit the rules by finding loopholes. This helps to explain why the Racing Rules of Sailing have become so long winded and complex. As an alternative, ISAF have attempted to formulate a simpler set of rules for novice racers known as 'Introductory Rules for Racing'. This concept was introduced as an experiment in 2008. Nothing is fundamentally different from the Racing Rules of Racing.

Some Explanations

Windward* and *Leeward*:** The *leeward* side of your boat is the side where your mainsail lies. The ***windward side is the other side.

***Port and Starboard Tack*:** You are on *port* or *starboard* tack according to your *windward* side.

***Advisor*:** A person appointed by race organisers to assist competitors in understanding the rules and, when appropriate, to penalise a boat.

Basic Rules

1. You must comply with the principles of good sportsmanship.

2. You must try not to collide with another boat.

Rules When Boats Meet

3. When you are sailing on ***port tack*** you must avoid boats on ***starboard tack***.

4. When you are sailing on the ***same tack***, you must avoid other boats which are:

   (a) in front of you.
   (b) on your *leeward* side.

5. When approaching a racing mark or obstacle (such as a moored yacht), any boats that are sailing between your boat and the mark or obstacle must be given sufficient space to pass it safely on the inside. However, if boats are on opposite tacks this rule does not apply. Starboard tack has right of way.

6. When another boat is required to keep clear of your boat, you must give the other boat adequate opportunity to take avoiding action.

Other Rules

7. At the starting signal you must be behind the starting line.

8. After the starting signal, you must sail the course described by the race organisers.

9. You must not touch a mark of the course.

10. If you think that your boat or another boat has broken a rule, or if you are unclear about the rules at any time during the race, you must describe the incident to the ***advisor*** after the race. The ***advisor*** may then add two points to the score of any boat that has broken a rule. If the offence is serious, the ***advisor*** may add extra points to the boat's score.

Responsibilities of Race Organisers

(a) To run fair, enjoyable and safe races.

(b) To inform all the competitors about the sequence of starting signals, the starting and finishing lines, the course to be sailed and the marks to be rounded.

(c) To score each boat points equal to her finishing position, after adjusting for handicaps when appropriate.

(d) To appoint an advisor on the rules and procedures for racing.

Introduction and Use

• These rules are designed to stand on their own so that sailors who are starting to race can compete without the need to learn the many details of the ISAF Racing Rules of Sailing (RRS). They are appropriate for small boats in sheltered waters; they are not intended for boats over 6 metres (20 feet) long.

• These rules are compatible with the principles and fundamental rules in the RRS. They omit as many complications of the RRS as possible, written for sailors who are starting to race or have no more than two years of racing experience, after which sailors should be encouraged to race under the RRS. Boats racing under these rules should race on their own course and not share the course area or marks with boats racing under the RRS.

• Unlike normal RRS, there is an obligation on the race organisers to verbally brief all competitors about the marks, the course and all relevant race management matters.

• The role of rules advisor is a vital part of teaching the rules. Ideally the rules advisor should be afloat and watch the racing but, as a minimum, the advisor must be available for discussion immediately the sailors return ashore. The rules advisor may be the same person as the race officer.

• The standard 2-place penalty for breaking a rule is small at this learning stage and avoids the difficulties of penalty turns. The 2-place penalty applies to all errors, although there is provision for increasing the penalty to avoid any advantage being gained.

The Bottom Line

• Good racing requires sportsmanship and decent behaviour.

• Avoid collisions by identifying responsibility on both sides.

• Dinghy racers learn rules through tactics – you need to discover what you can and cannot do. Always link tactics to racing rules.

• You are duty bound by the rules of racing to do everything possible to avoid hitting another boat. It is far better to sort out who is in the wrong in the protest room, rather than go through long winded insurance claims after a crash.

• If you are beating upwind and a collision appears imminent, push the helm away and crash tack or stop. Bearing away will accelerate the boat.

• Sailing downwind, it is vital that the crew scans all round, looking for traffic as visibility is drastically reduced when the spinnaker is flying. Bearing away early will clearly signal your intention to avoid a potential collision.

7 | Racing Courses

Dinghy racing should provide a mixture of beating, reaching and sailing downwind. The layout of the course is all important in providing a closely matched, exciting, tactical experience.

Windward-Leeward

High performance dinghies with asymmetric spinnakers are best suited to racing round courses with a windward/leeward format. The concept is simple, based around one leg to windward and one leg to leeward with any number of laps. Dinghies tack directly upwind to the windward mark, and then gybe downwind to the leeward mark on a series of reaches, which is considerably faster than sailing a direct course downwind. Sailing a longer distance at higher speed provides optimum VMG (Velocity Made Good), which equates to the true speed made towards your target. This is all thanks to the effects of apparent wind – the faster you sail on a reach, the deeper you can bear away downwind.

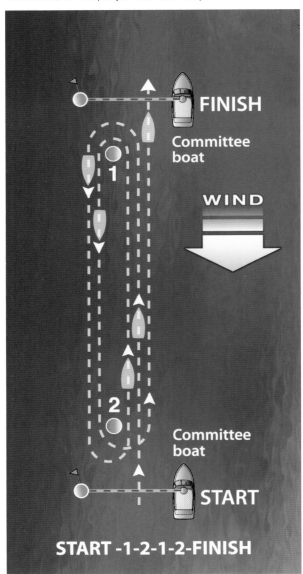

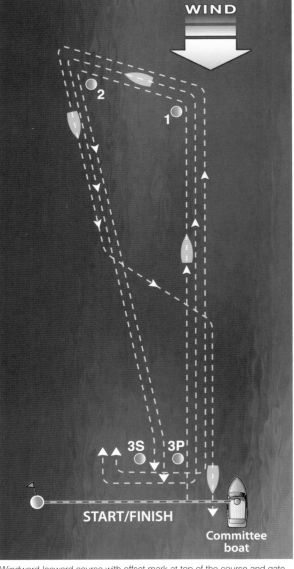

Basic windward-leeward course. The finish could also be at the bottom of the course, with boats crossing the line downwind.

Windward-leeward course with offset mark at top of the course and gate at bottom of the course to help separate boats at mark roundings.

The basic windward-leeward format provides the race committee with various options:
- Increasing or decreasing the number of laps.
- Deleting the final windward leg.
- Using a gate formed by two marks instead of a single leeward mark.
- Using an offset mark at the windward mark, to provide a short reach which separates boats sailing upwind and offwind at the top of the course.
- Using the leeward and windward marks as starting and finishing marks. An odd number of legs will provide a finish to windward; an even number of legs will provide a finish to leeward.

A windward-leeward race sequence might cover 2 or 3 laps of the course, with the race typically lasting up to 60 minutes:
- Start from the bottom of the course.
- Race directly upwind to Mark 1 (windward mark).
- Short reach to Mark 2 (offset spacer mark) about 50-75 metres distance and slightly upwind of Mark 1. This ensures that dinghies turning round Mark 2 and raising their spinnakers do not get in the way of port tack dinghies, which are still beating towards Mark 1 in a potentially crowded part of the course.
- Downwind to Gate Marks 3 or 4 which are rounded as port or starboard marks. Competitors can choose to turn round either mark, but must turn from the inside. This helps separate the fleet and prevent collisions.
- Back upwind to Mark 1.
- Short reach to Mark 2.

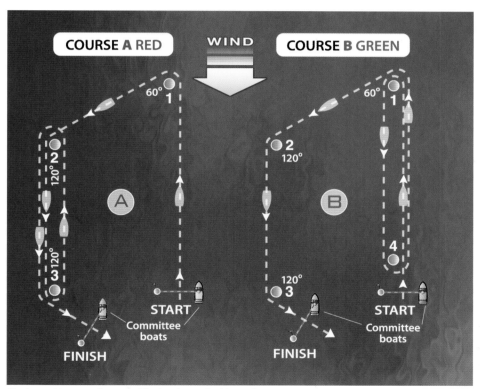

The trapezoid course allows a red fleet and green fleet to use the same course area.

Trapezoid

The trapezoid course provides a variation on the windward-leeward course, by using two windward-leeward courses which are connected by a tight reach at the top of the course – where flying a spinnaker will be difficult – and a broader reach at the bottom of the course which will allow boats to overtake. The principal advantage of this course is that different classes can be raced at the same time, by following a different sequence of inner and outer loops to keep them separated.

Options on a trapezoid course may include:
- Adding additional legs.
- Using gates instead of leeward marks for downwind legs.
- Varying the angles of the reaching legs. Typical angles for each turn of the course are 60-120-120.
- Using an offset mark at the beginning of downwind legs.
- Finish boats at the windward or leeward marks, rather than on a reach.

Windward-Leeward Triangle

The traditional racing course is the 'triangle and sausage' which provides beating, running and reaching. This format is ideal for classic dinghy classes and single-handers, since it provides equal emphasis on beating upwind and running directly downwind which is perfect with symmetrical spinnakers, as well as two reaches which can be sailed with and without spinnakers.

There are three marks of the course:

1. Windward mark at the top.
2. Wing mark out to the side.
3. Leeward mark at the bottom.

All marks must be rounded to port or starboard. The start is directly into the wind at the bottom of the course; the finish is directly into the wind at the top of the course. The number of laps and order of triangles or sausages are at the race officer's discretion.

Options might include:

1. Varying the angles of the triangle. Typical angles for each turn of the course are 45-90-45 or 60-60-60.
2. Deleting the last windward leg.
3. Using a gate instead of a leeward mark for downwind legs.
4. Using an offset mark at the beginning of downwind legs.
5. Using the leeward and windward marks as starting and finishing marks. An odd number of legs will provide a finish to leeward; an even number of legs will provide a finish to windward.

A typical race sequence might be:

• Start by Mark 3 at bottom of the course.
• Beat to Mark 1.
• Bear away for broad reach to Mark 2.
• Gybe for close reach to Mark 3 to complete triangle.

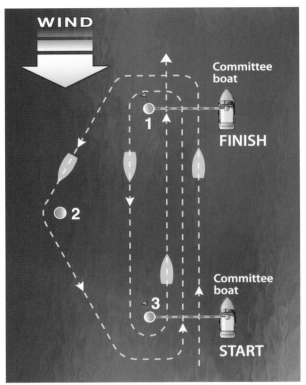

The classic windward-leeward triangle provides a long beat, long run and two shorter reaches.

• Head up to beat to Mark 1.
• Bear away or gybe to run downwind to Mark 3.
• Head up or gybe to beat to Mark 1 in order to complete sausage and cross the finish line.

Course options

Variations include rectangular and inverse 'P' courses (fig. A) which incorporate tight reaching and downwind sailing. In reality, many sailing clubs will use buoys and markers which are permanently in the water to set their courses, rather than laying marks to create a 'perfect' course. This means that while the course may be loosely based on windward and leeward sailing, the angles and distance of different legs will be extremely varied – more like an orienteering course!

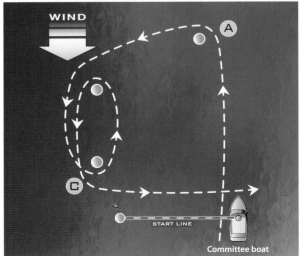

Fig. A: Beat, reach, run, beat, run and reach to the finish

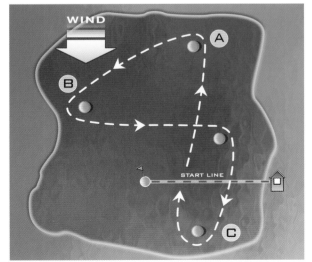

Inland clubs uses whatever space is available for an interesting course.

Sailing the course

- You must start; pass each mark on the required side in the correct order; and finish. This means that a string representing your boat's wake should lie on the required side of each mark when drawn taut. You may correct any errors to comply with this rule – normally by executing a penalty turn – provided you have not already finished.

- You finish when any part of your boat, crew or equipment (in its normal position) crosses the finishing line in the direction of the course from the last mark. You must complete any penalties, before finishing.

Insurance, Certificates and Class Membership

- Before you start racing, you will need third party insurance cover for your dinghy, in case of an accident while launching or afloat. This is mandatory for virtually all racing.

- Some classes require a measurement certificate, which confirms that the boat has been measured, weighed and possibly buoyancy tested to conform to class rules. This is not likely to be a requirement with modern one-design classes, which are effectively all the same.

- Joining the class association for your particular dinghy is strongly recommended. Class associations organise regular class events and training days. The class website is an excellent place to find news and information about your boat.

Before you go afloat

- You must wear a Personal Flotation Device to go racing. This is mandatory at most events – you will be disqualified if you don't wear one.

- A folding safety knife is not mandatory, but highly recommended. Best place to carry one is in the front pouch of your buoyancy aid.

- Make sure your boat is clean, with no big scratches or dents.

- Check the foils – daggerboard or centreboard and rudder blade – for damage. Make sure they can be raised or lowered without difficulty, and will stay locked down in position.

- Make sure all the sail controls are working, including control lines, cleats and shockcord tension.

- If the boat has a spinnaker, do a dry land hoist to ensure everything is correctly set up. It's not good to arrive at the windward mark first, ready to hoist your spinnaker upside-down or inside the forestay!

- Make sure the hull is completely drained of water, by tipping the boat and using a sponge. Then make sure inspection hatches and drain plugs are tightly closed.

- If you can alter mast rake, take a look at how the fast boats in your class have their rigs set up for the day's racing and refer to the class-tuning guide. This is normally available on class websites. Be aware that lighter crews will tend to need more rake to hold the boat upright.

- Check the rules for the race series. You may be required to carry a towline or paddle, or other safety gear. If you don't, you may be disqualified.

- How long do you expect to be out on the water? If races are held back-to-back (one after the other), it could be several hours. You will almost certainly need a bottle of water, which can be strapped to the mast, and some energy bars. Be prepared to get colder as the day progresses, particularly if you capsize. Always dress up, not down. If the boat has storage space, carry extra clothing such as spray tops which may be required if a light wind morning turns to a breezy afternoon.

- If sunny apply sunscreen.

- Have you got a watch with a count-down timer? Do you know how to work it? Precise timing is vital for a good start.

- Do not carry any extra weight on board. Light boats are fastest!

Check all sail controls to make sure nothing will break or come undone.

Make sure you don't hoist the spinnaker upside-down or inside the forestay!

Whatever you race, the objectives will be the same.

- Get round the course and finish the race.
- Do not hit other boats or incur penalties.
- Dinghy racing is a sport, which should be enjoyed amongst friends.
- Always treat your crew or helm with respect.
- Assess your performance and work out how to get a better result in the next race. Learn by your mistakes.

Ready to race and have fun at the Topper World Championship.

Team Racing

Team racing is popular with institutions such as universities and the armed forces. Events can either be BYOB (bring your own boat) or BP (boats provided). All the boats in a race must be the same class and reasonably well matched for performance. The Lark and Firefly have been favourite team racing classes.

Unlike fleet racing, where one boat wins, all the members of each team have their points score added together to determine the winning team, which may consist of two, three or four boats. Racing is highly tactical, since individual race winning doesn't count – instead you have to help ensure your team gets more points than their rivals. A team racing event comprises a number of races where the teams with the greatest number of wins progress onto the next stage of the competition. Races are ideally quite short – 10 to 15 minutes is adequate – and even events with hundreds of helms can be run with only 24 boats. Small events can be equally successful with just 4 or 6 boats and up to half a dozen teams.

More information: *www.teamracing.org*

The spoils of victory – it's great to win a regatta! These guys are celebrating at the end of the Topper World Championship.

Luck favours the well prepared. A series of checks will ensure you are ready to win the race.

The Hull

- The hull should be smooth to create minimum drag.

- Always wash the hull with fresh water to remove salt, dirt or stains. A coat of dinghy polish will make it harder for dirt to get a grip on the shiny surface.

- Smooth down small scratches with wet and dry sandpaper. Deep scratches need to be filled with gel coat and sanded to a perfect finish.

- Make sure there is no water inside the hull. Screw the drainage plug up tight and ensure all hatches are secure.

- Check that the gudgeons (rudder fittings attached to the transom) are totally rigid.

The Foils

- Ensure foils are perfectly smooth – fill and sand any dings in the rudder and centreboard or daggerboard. Pay particular attention to the trailing edge, which should be smooth and sharp.

- Make sure the rudder blade will lock fully down – if it is slightly lifted, you may get uncomfortable weather helm.

- The rudder blade must be a tight fit to ensure it will not flex in the stock.

- The tiller must be rigidly and securely attached to the head of the stock.

The Rig

- Check the connections at both ends of the shrouds and forestay. If you have a furling jib, be sure to double-check the top swivel for broken wire strands.

- Check for loose or cracked rivets and fittings on the mast and boom.

- Make sure all knots and split pins are secure. For extra security, wrap pins with a protective layer of insulating tape.

- Set the rig up with the correct amount of rake or pre-bend for the forecast conditions.

- Check battens for tension and batten pockets for wear.

The Controls

- Check for frayed ropes and over-stretched elastics. Replace if necessary. Make sure the ends of all ropes and control lines are sealed.

- Make sure all jamming cleats and ratchet blocks work perfectly. Spray on a dry lubricant for enhanced performance.

What will nature provide?

• Check the forecast wind speed and direction for morning and afternoon.

• Check where and when tide will be flowing on the course.

Dress up, not down

Wind chill ensures that it's always colder on the water. Be cautious and be prepared to cool down, particularly if you are racing back-to-back. If necessary, take extra clothing such as a spray top. Use sunscreen to provide maximum protection from the sun.

It can be cold holding a boat in the water. Make sure you are dressed for it. This photo was taken in February!

Time for food

Dinghy racers who want to win should eat a balanced, low fat diet with plenty of carbohydrates and protein, including lots of fruit and veg! If you are racing back-to-back, you should at least take some energy bars afloat.

'Water all around, and not a drop to drink...'

• Just like the ancient mariner, you will get dehydrated if you don't drink and your performance will deteriorate. The giveaway symptom is dark yellow urine, but by that stage it will take a long time to rehydrate.

vDrinking plain water can cause its own problems, because you need to urinate more frequently and natural salts are washed out of your body. Sports hydration drinks are designed to be more efficient, since the fluid will pass more slowly through your body. Alternatively, try drinking a mixture of half juice and half water for colder weather or one-third juice and two-thirds water for warmer weather.

Read and listen

• Read the Sailing Instructions which will specify all requirements for a series of races.

• Listen carefully to the Race Briefing before heading out to the start.

Launching for a race at the Topper World Championship on Lake Garda.

Dressed to Race | 9

Is the race going to be long, wet and cold or will it be warm and fast? Whatever the weather provides, you need to be racing in the perfect choice of clothing.

All dressed to win in the 'pro invitational' Volvo Champions race series in the 49er class.

9 | Dressed to Race

Flotation

A personal flotation device is normally mandatory for dinghy racing. A 50 Newton (10 Newtons = 1kg of flotation) personal flotation device is recommended for sailors weighing more than 70kg. Smaller sizes are suitable for lighter sailors including children, with flotation information clearly marked on a panel inside the personal flotation device.

- Choose a minimalist style personal flotation device, which pulls over your head with a side-entry zip. It should be the closest possible fit over your wetsuit, hikers or drysuit, with elasticised hem ensuring it stays snug and won't ride up, while your upper body and arms are virtually unrestricted. A zip or Velcro front pocket is a very useful feature. Make sure it is the correct size.

Foot protection

- Neoprene dinghy boots with rubber soles provide much more reliable grip than bare feet, whether you are hiking or trapezing. They also provide protection for feet and ankles when moving around the cockpit or launching the boat, with upper reinforcement to hold your feet securely under the toe strap. The boots must not roll on your feet when trapezing – this can be prevented by tensioning the Velcro straps across the uppers.

- Lighter weight neoprene shoes appear comfortable, but have limited use for summer racing. They do not provide the same level of protection and support as boots, and also tend to wear out much more quickly. Dinghy racing is surprisingly tough on your feet!

Hand Protection

- If you are to get a strong grip on synthetic sheets and control lines, hand protection is vital. Repeatedly trimming the mainsheet soon takes its toll, and you won't win races if you're slow hauling on the halyard or retrieval line during spinnaker hoists and drops.

- Standard sailing gloves have strongly reinforced, synthetic leather, non-slip palms. They also have lightweight mesh backs for quick draining, Velcro wrist straps for precise fit and short fingers for picking out lines. Make sure the gloves feel comfortable and that you can bunch each hand tightly enough to grip a narrow diameter control line – if not, those gloves will become progressively more uncomfortable.

- An interesting alternative is provided by Crewsaver Response gloves with Nitrile rubber coated palm and fingers. They are exceptionally light, grippy and comfortable to wear, but may only last one race before they start to deteriorate. So it's as well they are cheap to buy!

Head protection

- A peaked cap will help cut dazzle on a sunny day, which may make it easier to spot the next mark. It will also provide some protection against spray or rain getting into your eyes.

- If the weather is cold, a thermal beanie provides first class protection against heat loss from your head and should also be relatively spray-proof.

Eye protection

Glare on the water can be a big problem when racing on a sunny day. A good pair of polarized sunglasses will provide much improved vision, as well as protecting against UV. Choose a close fitting, floatable frame and attach a head-strap retainer if you don't want to lose them. But if salt spray builds up on the lenses, take them off or you won't be able to see anything!

Skin protection

Racing concentrates the mind. So much so that you may forget about the effects of sun, especially when there is a cooling breeze. Always protect exposed skin with high factor, water resistant sunscreen before you hit the water. If you are racing back-to-back, take the sunscreen afloat and reapply liberally between races.

Cutting through

When you race, it's a wise precaution to carry a safety knife or stainless steel multi tool. The pocket on the front of a personal flotation device can provide the perfect storage solution.

Almost dry

A wetsuit can provide the perfect all-round sailing solution, with the addition of a dry top or spray top worn for colder weather.

- Dinghy racing requires unrestricted upper body movement. Choose a short arm steamer (wetsuit with sealed seams) or long john for warmer weather. The neck must be supple enough to get your head out of the boat and look around the course without restriction. Legs and arms must be able to flex freely, with thicker neoprene in the main body of the wetsuit providing necessary core warmth.

- Thickness of neoprene determines warmth, which also depends on a very close fit with watertight seams and zip to prevent cold water flushing through the suit and lowering your body temperature. Wetsuits for winter use will typically use 5 mm neoprene for the body and legs with 3 mm for arms and shoulders which require extra mobility. For summer use, 3 mm neoprene will suffice and make the suit considerably lighter and more flexible.

- When choosing a wetsuit a perfect fit is vital. All wetsuits have a Lycra inner lining to make the neoprene easier to pull on and off your body. This also relies on the stretchiness of the neoprene – a super stretchy suit will pull on and off like a glove. Make sure you can operate the rear entry zip unassisted – some zips are easier to pull than others!

- Avoid smooth skin neoprene, which is vulnerable to cuts and abrasion. Reinforced knee patches are vital if you spend any time kneeling in the cockpit in lighter winds.

- Wear a harness for trapezing or hiking shorts on top of the wetsuit for added protection around the seat and at the back of the thighs. Your wetsuit will last a lot longer!

- A good quality wetsuit will last for many years with basic maintenance. Always wash the wetsuit in fresh water after salt water use, ensuring salt does not build up in the zip. Allow the suit to dry and store in a cool, dark place on a plastic hanger. Do not leave the suit folded or crumpled and keep it out of direct sunlight. Small tears in the neoprene can be repaired with super-glue. Since the wetsuit is worn next to your body, personal hygiene is important – a maltreated wetsuit can become a bacteria-ridden garment!

Upper body movement is vital for trimming sheets – a short sleeve wetsuit provides the best solution for racing through the summer season.

Totally dry

A drysuit will keep you warm and dry when worn with a synthetic thermal base layer, which makes it a good investment for a winter series. The downside is that drysuits tend to be cumbersome, partly due to the necessity for a heavy duty, waterproof zip.

Getting wet doesn't matter if you wear a drysuit with effective seals.

- Choose a drysuit which is as tight fitting as possible, but will still allow you to bend and stretch in all directions with the air expelled. Breathable material is top choice, although expensive. Remember that the breathable concept will not function perfectly unless you also wear breathable layers underneath or on top.

- A diagonal zip across the front makes it a lot easier to get in and out of the suit, but a horizontal zip across the back tends to feel more comfortable when worn with a trapeze harness.

- Latex socks are recommended to keep the water out of your feet and are much easier to get into and out of than ankle seals. Neoprene neck and wrist seals do not provide such an efficient waterproof seal as latex, but are a lot more comfortable and much less likely to rip.

- Drysuits are expensive so treat them with care. Wash off salt and store the drysuit on a plastic hanger in a cool, dark environment. Treat seals with a proprietary lubricant at regular intervals. Be aware that latex seals will eventually perish. If a seal fails when you are sailing, it will surely be unpleasant and could be dangerous as your drysuit fills with water. Replacing seals before it's too late is an inexpensive and straightforward operation. The drysuit zip needs a regular wash with fresh water. An occasional rub with candle wax will ensure smooth sliding – you can briefly melt the wax into the teeth with a hair dryer. Drysuits are damaged by overexposure to direct sunlight or heat. Leaving a drysuit on the rear shelf of your car is not recommended!

Totally dry for comfortable winter sailing. This photo was taken in the UK in January, but these Cadet sailors are still having a great time!

Hiking pleasure

* Hikers are designed to help take the pain out of hiking, with battens or pads to spread the load when the back of your legs are pressed against the deck. This would normally restrict blood flow and helps explain the intense discomfort you might feel on a long beat to windward.

* Battens and pads need to be perfectly positioned for hiking flat out or closer in to the boat, and must not move around when you are out on the side.

* Hikers can be worn as a pair of hiking pants on top of a wetsuit, or as neoprene hikers with three-quarter length legs and shoulder straps, which combines a wetsuit with hiking pants in one garment. This provides the almost perfect solution for many dinghy racers. Add a spray top or dry top for extra protection from wind and water, with the option of wearing thermal layers underneath to stay warm in colder weather.

"Grrrr..." Wear 'hikers' if you want to make hiking a pleasure. Alison Young races ahead in a Laser Radial.

Top protection

* A spray top can be worn over the top of a wetsuit or hikers, for additional protection against spray and wind. If your dinghy has storage space, a spray top weighs almost nothing and should be taken afloat, providing the option of adding a layer while waiting – and getting colder – between races.

* A dry top does all the same things as a spray top, but has tighter neoprene seals at the neck and wrists, which will keep water out – unless you capsize. It will feel more restrictive but is top choice for colder weather, particularly when wearing thermal layers which need to be kept dry underneath.

A spray top or dry top provides protection against wind and water, while allowing free upper body movement.

Trapeze harness

- A trapeze harness has to be comfortable for the whole race or race series. There are pressure points where the hook pulls forward on your hips, and your back needs extra support for trapezing in high performance, flat-out fashion.

- Most harnesses have straps across the shoulders and adjusters across the hips to keep the hook close to your body – the hook should not pull away which will pressurise your hips. Thick padding around the seat and hips makes the harness more comfortable, while helping to comply with the ISAF rule that a harness should provide positive buoyancy.

- To spread the load of the hook, an aluminium or tough plastic spreader bar is widely favoured in conjunction with an array of adjustable straps. However, simple solutions can work well. The old style of harness, with a hook mounted on a small central plate, has to be laced tightly like a corset but may provide the most comfortable harness solution of all.

- The harness should fit snugly over a wetsuit or drysuit. Your personal flotation device is worn over the top and must be high enough to provide clear access to the hook.

- Do not leave the ends of the straps flapping around. Tuck them away, or cut them off if they are definitely too long. There is normally a quick-release buckle at the side of the harness, so you can theoretically wriggle out of the harness in a hurry. In practice, this does not provide a failsafe solution if you are trapped by the hook.

Just hang in there… no matter how wet you get. These guys are having a very wet ride on this RS800. Maybe they should try a shorter trapeze wire length?

Rash vest

A rash vest will tidy your profile. Wear it on top of everything to reduce windage and prevent bits of the trapeze harness or buoyancy aid from snagging when you tack, gybe or capsize. It's a great way to look both neat and cool.

Rash vests are cool – just like this Magic Marine duet on an RS800.

10 | Starting

The start can be the most critical (and stressful) part of a race. Boats that cross the line fast, with nothing to obstruct their wind, are already well placed to win.

Sail your boat as fast as possible and hike for your life! Getting a clean start will have a critical effect on the rest of the race. This is the Laser Radial class starting at the World Sailing Championships in Cascais, Portugal.

10 Starting

Marking the line

The start line is sighted between two points, often marked by the mast of a committee boat at the starboard end and a prominent outer limit mark at the port end. Some sailing clubs may start races from a fixed starting platform or from the shore, when transits (such as two white posts) may be used to indicate the line.

The committee boat marks the end of the line for an RS200 start on Lake Garda.

Start line length

The start line should ideally be equal to the length of all the boats + 25-50% to provide a safety margin for different conditions. In theory, the bow of every boat should be able to cross the start line at the same moment.

A short line provides a dynamic start for 49ers on the Volvo Champions circuit.

Start line angle

- To achieve a perfectly fair start for all competitors, the race committee will lay a line that is approximately at 90 degrees to the wind so that both ends are equally close to the windward mark and neither end is favoured. This will provide a direct beat to windward, which will separate the fleet on both sides of the course as they race towards the first mark. The wind may keep shifting in direction before the start, in which case the race committee may need to keep changing the angle of the line. This can lead to a frustrating wait for competitors.

- The angle of the start line may be changed to move the outer limit mark slightly upwind. A start line with a very small amount of port bias helps to draw the fleet down the full length of the line and avoid pile-ups around the committee boat and premature starts. A bias of 5 to 10 degrees works well.

- If the line has a strong port bias, it may be possible to get a flying start on port tack which crosses the majority of the fleet on starboard tack. However, crews who try port flyers need a low heart rate and paid-up insurance policy! The door is often shut firmly on them by starboard tackers who get their time and distance right at the gun, while fighting for the pin and pole position.

- In some circumstances, a reaching or downwind start may be used. This creates the obvious problem that competitors' sails will be blanketed from the side or behind.

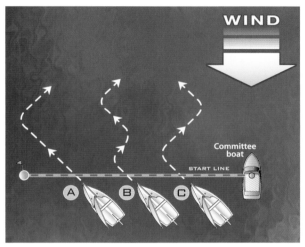

Start line is square to the wind. A, B, and C all have the same distance to sail to the windward mark.

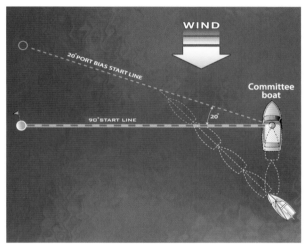

The start line is biased to port. A is closer to the windward mark and ahead of B when they cross the line.

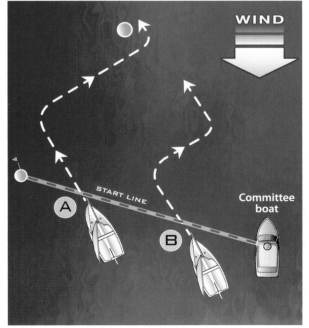

The start line has a 20 degree port end bias. Racers starting near the committee boat have extra distance to cross the line.

Leave time before the start to check line bias.

Hitting the line on the start gun requires great skill. Boats in the 'second row' are already being pushed down the fleet and will find it difficult to recover.

Start sequences (Racing Rules 26)

The standard start sequence is:

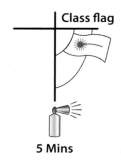

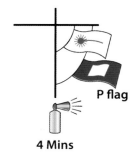

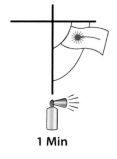

5 minutes: Class Flag is hoisted on the committee boat + sound signal.

4 minutes: Code Flag P (Blue Peter) 'preparatory flag' is hoisted + sound signal.

1 minute: Code Flag P is lowered + sound signal.

0 minutes: Class Flag is lowered + sound signal.

Timing the start

- Use a splash-proof watch with a countdown which can be synchronised with the 5-minute warning or 4-minute preparatory signals.
- For best performance, invest in a digital regatta timer with a large display and sound signals for the count down. This can be worn on your wrist or mounted on the boat. It can also be combined with a digital compass.

Making a perfect start

The aims of a good start are:

- Cross the start line at the most advantageous point immediately after the start signal.
- Start sailing at full speed as soon as possible.
- Follow the most efficient route upwind, without being hindered by other boats – it is vital to keep clear of other boats' wind shadows, which will slow you down and push your boat below the optimum course to windward.

Top 49er racers achieve almost perfect sychronisation, with equal advantage as four boats leave the start.

Start management

- Starting is often the most demanding part of the race. The aim is for your bows to hit the line as the start gun goes, sailing at full speed with no boats ahead so you have clean air and can point high upwind. This requires experience, expertise and a very cool head while all around are jostling for position.

- On a double-handed boat, the crew will usually take responsibility for timing the start, checking the committee boat flags and using a watch that provides reliable countdown information. The crew should also check tide. Just drop something that floats by a mark and note which way it floats. Beware of a strong current that may sweep you over the start line or against the windward/leeward mark.

- Prior to the start, check the boat is correctly set up for racing. Cross the line beating to windward at full power and put in a tack. Spot the windward mark if possible. Sail back downwind to practise a spinnaker hoist (if applicable) and gybe.

Keep up! Cadets drift towards the port end of the line in the last minute before the start.

Cadets sail along the line on starboard tack in the last seconds before they head up to cross for the start.

Where to start

- The whole fleet will normally start on starboard tack, with a natural tendency to bunch up by the committee boat. Starting from the committee boat end has the advantage that you can tack onto port soon after the start, to avoid dirty wind from other boats. This reduces the chance of losing out due to a poor start.

- It is occasionally possible to start from the outer end of the line with a port tack flyer that crosses in front of the starboard tack fleet. This high-risk strategy relies on start line bias that strongly favours the outer end.

- The angle between the start line and wind direction decides if one end is favoured. The start line should be square to the wind, but there will normally be some bias – possibly caused by a late shift in wind direction.

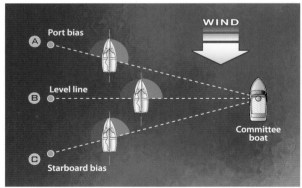

How to decide where to start. Sail along the line and turn the boat head to wind. If the bow points to port, the port end is favoured. If the bow points to starboard, the starboard end is favoured. If the bow points straight ahead, the line is at right angles to the wind.

- To assess bias, sail onto the line and turn the boat directly into the wind. If it points towards one end of the line – committee boat or outer limit mark – that end is favoured. Alternatively, sail along the line in both directions with your mainsail right out. This will show if either end of the line is further upwind and therefore closer to the first mark, making it the favourable end to start from.

- A fleet of boats will often sag in the middle as it crosses the line. Crews at either end have the committee boat or outer limit mark to show when they are to the line, which allows them to power off the line the moment the gun is fired. Crews starting from the middle hold back, because they are not sure if they have reached the line. It is possible to use landmarks for reference to confirm the line's position.

Lining up and holding position during the RS Feva National Championships.

Holding position on the line

- The object is to hold your position close to the line on starboard tack, without being blown sideways. This will help ensure you have enough space to accelerate towards the line for the start, without needing to pinch to avoid the boat to leeward which will have right of way. Pinching will slow your boat and immediately drop it into dirty wind from faster boats on the windward side, plus you will get dirty wind from that leeward boat accelerating ahead as well.

- Ease off the kicking strap to depower the mainsail. Keep the boat upright to ensure the board provides maximum resistance to sideslip. Point the bows towards the wind on a beating course to prevent moving ahead.

Keeping clear

- A major problem at the start is the turbulence and blanketing effect from other boats. Boats in the front row have clear wind and get away fast. Boats behind cannot point high or sail as fast due to dirty wind. In a crowded fleet this problem may persist for some distance on the first leg of the race. Once clear of the start, boats in dirty wind will have to tack to sail in clean air.

- If possible, keep a space to leeward so you can sail free and accelerate at the start. Boats that are forced to point high will get rolled over by boats sailing across the line at full blast.

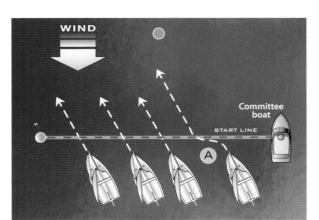

Leave room to leeward to bear away and accelerate towards the line, ensuring the boat hits it at full speed. This will enable you to pull ahead of slower boats and ensure you start the beat with clean wind.

Crossing the line

- In fresh winds it pays to cross the line at full speed. As the final countdown approaches, take up a position around 50 metres behind the committee boat end of the line. Spot a perfect gap on the line to accelerate through in the last 30 seconds.

- It only pays to sit on the line if the wind is so light that it would not be possible to accelerate through a gap. You must defend your position on the line, holding the boat stationary by pushing out the mainsail and backing the jib. This can also be used to change heading, ready to sheet in and go in the last 10 seconds.

- Do not get pushed over the line just before the start. In the final countdown it's typical for boats to line up in a waiting position ready to accelerate towards the start line. Boats are very close together and may drift very close to the line. If you start drifting over the line, you cannot bear away when a boat to leeward is obstructing your passage – you are the windward boat and you must keep clear. The only solution is to sail over the line, go round the end and rejoin the starters with little chance of a good position.

Hit the line at full speed, but don't hit the boat which is marking the end! If it's too crowded, remember that boats windward cannot push you down.

Are you on the line?

If the start line is crowded with boats, it can be very difficult to judge how close you are to the line. As boats line up, they have a tendency to hang back in a curve with most starting late. One solution is to identify a fixed object, such as a tree or moored yacht, which will provide a transit when your are exactly on the line. Be aware that the bows must not be over the line before the start.

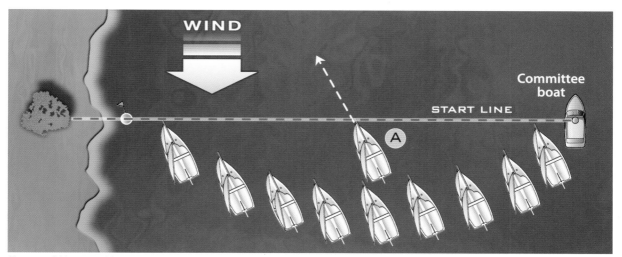

The crew of A have used the tree as a transit to identify when their bow is on the line. This enables them to cross the line first, while other boats are hanging back because they are not sure exactly where their line is.

Lots of space at the outer end – 45438 is about to cross the line at full speed in clean air during the Topper Championships on Lake Garda.

10 Starting

Start recalls

At the starting signal, your boat must be completely on the pre-start side of the starting line. If it is not, you must return and start correctly, while keeping clear of all boats that have started. The race committee will notify anyone who starts too early.

RRS 29.1 Individual Recall: Used when any part of the boat is over the line on course side (OCS). The boat may dip back over the line to be on pre-start side. Code Flag X is flown for individual recalls with one sound signal. The Race Officer must sound and raise flag quickly.

RRS 29.2 General Recall: First Substitute (general recall) is flown with two sound signals to bring all the fleet back. Usually lowered with one sound signal, one minute before the Class Flag to start the sequence again.

RRS 30.1 I Flag Rule: Code Flag I is flown instead of Code Flag P with the same time sequence – up at 4 minutes and down at 1 minute before start. Any boat OCS within 1 minute of start must go around the ends to restart.

RRS 30.2. Z Flag Rule: If Code flag Z is flown instead of P, any boat OCS within 1 minute of the start will have its score reduced by 20% penalty.

RRS 30.3. Black Flag Rule: Black flag used instead of Code Flag P. Any boat OCS within 1 minute of start is disqualified (DSQ) without hearing.

Gate starts

A gate start can be used to start a big fleet of identical boats, with the advantage that no boat can prematurely cross the line. This system is used for major RS regattas.

- One crew is nominated to sail the Pathfinder boat. Typically, the race organiser may choose the crew who finish 10th in the previous race.

- At 15 seconds before the starting signal, the Pathfinder starts sailing close-hauled on port tack, starting from within one boat length of the starting mark, which is laid at the leeward end of the starting gate.

- The starting line for all boats except the Pathfinder is between the starting mark and the centre of the stern of the Gate Launch, which follows closely behind the Pathfinder.

- All other boats start by crossing the starting line on starboard tack, after the starting signal and before the gate closes. Any boat which crosses the starting line between the one-minute signal and the starting signal is disqualified.

- A Guard Launch can be used to protect the Pathfinder from collisions, by keeping station off her starboard bow.

- The Pathfinder will stay close-hauled on port tack for a minimum of two minutes, before being released by the Gate Launch. The crew of the Pathfinder may then start the race, by tacking onto starboard tack.

- The Gate Launch continues on the same course at the same speed, until the end of the period of time displayed on the Committee Boat. At that point, the Gate Launch will stop its engines and the flag 'G' is lowered, indicating the closing of the gate.

Top Tips

- Port tack must give way to starboard tack. With a lot of boats close together, it is normally much easier and safer to start on starboard tack.

- A windward boat must keep clear of a leeward boat. You cannot bear down on a boat to leeward, in an effort to avoid crossing the line too early.

- Allow room to accelerate to full speed in the final approach to the line.

- Aim to start in clean air, as far away from other boats as possible.

- Beware of tide sweeping you across the line before the start.

- Learn to handle the boat so you can stay on the line, manoeuvre in a tight space or reverse away.

Pick your spot to cross the line paying attention to other boats. Only leeward boats can bear away.

Sheet in and power up for the final approach. The leeward boat can luff onto a proper course.

Full speed as your bow hits the line on the start signal – not a second earlier or later!

11 | Racing Upwind

The object is to reach the windward mark as quickly as possible. This means you need to be sailing at maximum speed, using wind which is blowing in the most advantageous direction, while keeping clear of 'wind shadow' created by other boats.

Welcome to the M25...
470 action during Hyeres Sailing Week.

Go for speed

- Leave the line at full speed to get clear of other boats. Extra effort in the first 60 seconds after the start can put you in clean air and allow you to tack without other boats blocking the way.

- Choose the best compromise between speed through the water and pointing upwind to maximise VMG, which is your true speed towards the windward mark. How high you can point will depend on the type of boat you are racing. Modern skiff-style designs tend to be most efficient when they are sailed free and fast on the beat, with the ability to plane to windward. Pinching into the wind will cause them to stall.

- Some dinghies tack very quickly. It may be possible to tack a Laser and accelerate back up to speed in little more than 15 seconds, but only if you have sufficiently good technique. Other dinghies tack quite slowly, in which case tacks should be kept to a minimum, dictated by major wind shifts rather than temporary lulls or tacking to avoid dirty wind from another boat.

Wind shadow

- When beating to windward, dirty wind will be created by another boat directly ahead, or slightly ahead on the windward or leeward side of your bows. The result will be increased turbulence and less pressure on your sails, with the result that it not only slows down but also points lower.

- If the boat creating wind shadow is being sailed badly, for instance pinching into the wind or heeling over too far, you may be able to power through its wind shadow at higher speed. But in most situations you are stuffed! The only solution is to tack out of the wind shadow as soon as possible.

- Dirty wind is a big problem for boats that don't cross the start line first. You will not be able to tack out of trouble since there will generally be a mass of starboard tack boats immediately to windward. Watch and wait for a gap, and then tack into it without delay. Never continue sailing in dirty wind any longer than you have to.

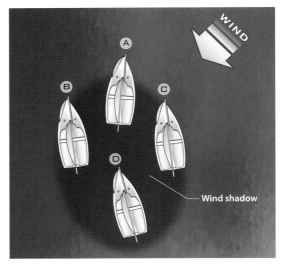

B and C are both affected by wind shadow from A. D is affected by wind shadow from all three boats. The solution is to tack into clear wind.

If you're racing a skiff style boat like this RS800, you've got to sail fast and free and hold the boat flat, with minimum tacks..

Covering

- Covering is a tactic to ensure a rival boat cannot overtake. It is often used in the final stages of a race or championship, when a leading boat might cover its main challenger with the intention of keeping it down the fleet for the duration of the race. The theory of covering is easy, but practice relies on both crews having equal boat handling skills.

- Boat A positions itself to windward and ahead of boat B which is stuck in its wind shadow. Boat B therefore tacks to break the cover. Boat A immediately tacks to restore the cover. This process can also be repeated on downwind legs. The obvious drawback is that other boats may get ahead. However this may be irrelevant when a championship is being decided between the two contenders.

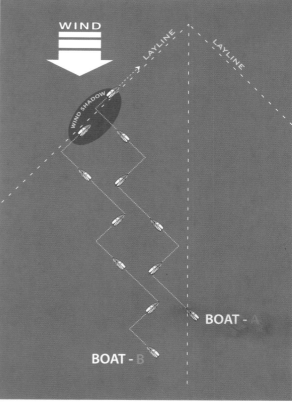

GBR 8542 can cover every tack of the blue boat.

A tacks to cover B all the way up the beat. B is stuck in A's wind shadow on the lay line approach to the windward mark.

The nearest Laser boat can't point, because it is sailing in dirty wind coming off the windward side of the leading boat's sail. The only solution is to tack.

Wind shifts

If the wind is fickle, standard advice is to keep reasonably close to the rhumb line which is the direct route from the start to the windward mark.

- If the wind shifts to the right, the right side of the course will be favoured. If the wind shifts to the left, the left side of the course will be favoured.

A Laser tacks fast – be ready to tack if the wind heads you and makes the boat bear away.

Racing through waves

- Each wave provides an obstacle, which your boat has to sail over or break through as it races upwind. The most difficult waves to maintain speed through are closely spaced and steep, typically when wind is blowing directly against the tidal flow. Bear off a few degrees to ensure the boat keeps powering ahead, instead of stalling when the bows hit each wave.

- When the boat is lifted by a wave, it may be suddenly exposed to stronger, cleaner wind and heel over. Be prepared to depower on the top of the wave by easing the mainsail.

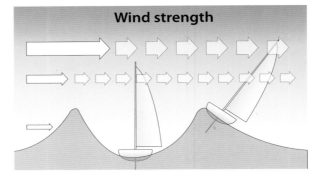

Wind strength

Hike hard and lift your body over the waves. Charlotte Dobson shows that sailing can be a very tough sport.

Managing the Start and the First Beat

Leading dinghy racing coach and sailmaker Michael McNamara passes on his training tips between the start and first leg of a race.

- The bigger the fleet, the more important it is to get away cleanly at the start and to get the first beat right. To do this consistently, sailors not only need good technique but also require strategical and tactical awareness.

- Technique is vital not only in getting the boat going fast through the water, but also helps when the sailor is under pressure from opposition boats. It means the boat should always be positively and accurately controlled, almost without conscious effort. The sailor is then left free to concentrate both on going the right way and coping with other boats on the race course.

- The strategy of going the right way can be defined as using the environment to get to the windward mark as quickly as possible. It therefore relies on long term planning. This comes both from experience and from lessons learnt immediately before the start, when preparing for the race.

- Tactics needed to cope with other boats rely on a knowledge of the Racing Rules, as well as the ability to think quickly enough to make the right immediate decisions – the emphasis is much more short term.

The relationship between technique, strategy and tactics will vary during the beat, depending on which has priority at any moment.

The Start

- Before the warning signal, plan the strategy of the beat by working out what is happening to the wind and tidal currents. By sailing for some distance on each tack, a pattern will emerge of where the wind will be steady or varying in both direction and speed. More usually, the wind will be oscillating from side to side about a mean direction, although there could be a gentle but progressive variation in direction known as a wind bend. Timing of the shifts and working out the change in the wind is vital. You will also need to work out which end of the starting line is favoured and sort out rig settings.

- At the warning signal, make sure of the timing and decide which end to start.

- At the prepatory signal, focus completely on the start. Double check rig settings and check for weed on the rudder.

- At the one-minute signal, be in position and vigorously defend as well as getting ready to start.

- In the last few seconds, get up to full acceleration and GO!

- In the minute after the start, nothing else matters but speed. Keep the boat flat and driving, watching out for waves that could stop the boat.

McNamara sails in upwind action.

First Quarter of the Beat

- In oscillating wind conditions, get on the correct swing as soon as possible, even if it means ducking other boat's sterns to get to the best side.

- If the wind is not varying, then boat speed is most important as it will not matter where the boat is on the course.

- If a permanent wind bend is detected, take the heading tack even if it means ducking sterns. Then tack short of the lay line, because the wind bend may lift the boat up to the windward mark on the new tack.

Last Three-Quarters of the Beat

- Always under tack a bunch of boats.

- Do not sail away from the fleet.

- Think twice if you are on the opposite tack to the majority of boats. However, remember that a boat on the opposite tack to the leading group will be less affected by their dirty wind.

- Do not get out to the starboard lay line early. That long parade in towards the mark can be both frustrating and slow.

- Only approach the windward mark on port tack if you are in the leading group, or when the starboard tack boats are being severely headed by a wind shift.

- Approach the mark at least a boom width to windward, especially if there are waves.

At the end of the beat to windward, you will reach the windward mark. Here you will bear away to sail the next leg of the race, either directly downwind or on a reach…

Follow my leader. The lay line leads directly to the mark. If you are too far to leeward, you won't make it, not least because windward boats will mess up your wind.

op of the Course

line

After making its final tack, a boat should be able to sail directly towards the windward mark. This course is known as the lay line, meaning that you can lay the mark.

- The final approach to the windward mark should be relatively short to allow for wind shifts and the effects of tide. In most races the windward mark must be left to port, so for maximum safety the final approach should always be made on starboard tack. Approaching on port tack, which must give way, is a high-risk venture when there are boats approaching on starboard.

- Unless you are leading, other boats will be going round the mark at the same time. This will create an area of disturbed air in which you may not be able to sail fast or point high and consequently get pushed down onto the mark. Approach with enough room to leeward to allow for loss of power or dodging other boats, without going so far upwind that you have to reach down to the mark.

Coming in very tight on the lay line!

Rule breakers

Beware the overlap rule when approaching the windward mark on the lay line. If the inside boat has established an overlap before the zone, it must be given sufficient room to round the mark. Do not sail into a space on the inside of another boat within zone of a mark.

Boats approaching within three boat lengths of a mark. Remember that boats approaching on starboard tack will have right of way. .

B goes behind A and tacks onto starboard.

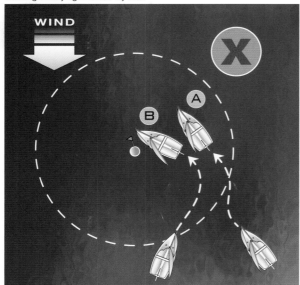

B tacks onto starboard inside A, but forces A to luff above close hauled. B must therefore take a penalty.

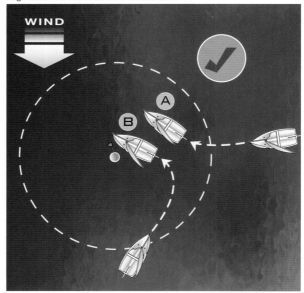

B tacks onto starboard inside A. This is allowed, since A only has to luff to close hauled to avoid B.

The final tack

• If you tack too late, you will over stand the mark and are likely to lose out to boats which are directly on the lay line.

• If you tack too early, you will need to pinch which will slow the boat down. If all goes well, you may be able to squeeze safely round the mark – remember that you cannot hit it! But in many situations, dirty wind created by boats which are sailing in on the lay line will mean that you cannot point high. If you fail to sail up to the lay line, which is likely, you will be forced to tack again. This usually means tacking onto port and having to avoid a stream of starboard tack boats making their final approach. Not recommended!

• Tacking too early can cause big problems in a light breeze, since the boat will not have the power to drive upwind and will suffer particularly badly from the effects of dirty wind.

The leading Laser is forced to tack for the mark by a starboard tack boat. This is not good if you are below the lay line and have to pinch to lay the mark.

Tidal flow

Be aware of tidal flow. If the flow is upwind, you will be able to tack early or risk over standing the mark. If the flow is downwind, you will need to tack late, with careful judgment of how far the tide will carry your boat sideways on the final approach to the mark. This problem will be severe if there is a foul tide, carrying your boat downwind of the mark.

Over standing the mark is safe, but loses metres.

Bearing away round the mark

- Ease the kicking strap before you bear way round the mark. If you need to raise the centreboard or daggerboard, do so after you bear away.

- Keep the boat flat or heel it slightly to windward as you bear away. If the boat heels to leeward, its natural tendency will be to keep heading upwind, which is where you don't want to go!

- You will need to ease the mainsheet to bear away – do not let the end of the boom hit the mark. (If you want to do something really embarrassing, it's possible to lasso the mark and get totally hog-tied!)

- Keep watching what's going on around you, while bearing away. You must keep clear of boats to leeward.

1. Bear away with the kicking strap eased.

2. Heel the boat slightly to leeward. Do not let the boom hit the mark!

3. Concentrate on steering as you bear right away.

45197 and 45159 start bearing away offwind, with boats still approaching the mark.

Where to next?

- Locate the next buoy before you get to the windward mark, so you are ready to turn straight onto the new course.

- If there is a single windward mark, the course change will effectively require a 180-degree turn. You will bear away downwind, with the option of a gybe to get clear of following boats. Beware of other boats still beating towards the windward mark on starboard tack. If you are sailing downwind on port tack, you must also give way to port tack boats sailing upwind.

- If the windward mark is followed by an offset spacer mark, the course change will be approximately 90 degrees, providing a beam reach across the top of the course. This separates boats which have already rounded the windward mark from boats which are still approaching.

Spot the next mark as you turn. This Laser has missed the opportunity to gybe inside the leader, which could have provided a windward advantage.

Be cautious with the kite!

The spacer leg across the top of the course is a beam reach. It may be deep enough to hoist the spinnaker, providing extra power to blast past boats which have not gone for the hoist. This may work beautifully in lighter winds, but in stronger winds there are two good reasons to be cautious!

1. You need to hold the boat flat and bear away deep enough to hoist the kite, which may not be possible with boats sailing to leeward. (On a twin wire boat such as the 49er or RS800, the helm can stay on the trapeze while the crew hoists the kite from the cockpit.)

2. If you have to bear away to hold the boat flat in gusts with the spinnaker, you may not be able to sail high enough to avoid boats to leeward. Even worse, you may not be able to sail high enough to make it round the spacer mark. The only solution is to bear away and drop the kite, then beat back to the spacer mark while avoiding other boats zipping across on starboard tack. This is an excellent (and embarrassing) way to lose a lot more places in the race!

Trying to sail high with the kite can be dangerous. If a gust hits, you are at the mercy of more cautious boats.

13 | Racing Downwind

Racing downwind provides the fastest part of the race, running or reaching all the way back down to the leeward mark at the bottom of the course...

RS Fevas use windy conditions on Lake Garda to sail as deep as possible, maintaining a balance between speed and course downwind.

Direct to the leeward mark

- Dinghies with symmetrical spinnakers like the Cadets below, or single-handed dinghies such as the Laser, will be optimised for VMG by sailing directly downwind towards the leeward mark. Sailing by the lee (bearing away past a dead run, so the wind blows over the leeward side of the stern) will enable a more direct course, with the possibility of no gybe until you reach the leeward mark.

Cadets race directly downwind during the Eric Twiname Championship event on Rutland water.

- On a windward-leeward course, the second major leg of the race is directly downwind. In most situations, dinghies with asymmetric spinnakers will be optimised for VMG (velocity made good towards the leeward mark) by sailing from reach to reach, tacking back down the course with a series of gybes.

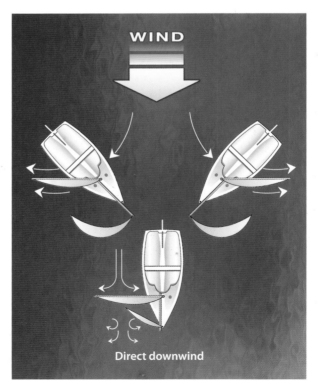

Asymmetric dinghies sail further and faster on a series of reaches toward the leeward mark.

Leave room to leeward to sail deep to hoist the kite, then luff to build up speed.

Go for speed with an asymmetric

- Skiff-style dinghies sail on apparent wind. Luff up to build power in lulls, and then bear away to sail deep on the apparent wind which not only increases but also moves ahead. Always keep the boat flat. If you let the boat heel over to leeward, it will want to turn up towards the true wind.

- The faster the boat goes, the deeper downwind it can sail, reducing the distance to the leeward mark. If the breeze is strong, you can sail at approximately 135 degrees to the true wind direction for the best compromise between speed and VMG. If the breeze is light, you will not be able to sail deep. Some dinghies, such as the RS400, have a control known as a wing-wang which pulls the end of the spinnaker pole to the windward side of the bows. This allows the boat to sail deeper downwind, without the mainsail blanketing and collapsing the spinnaker.

A perfectly trimmed boat allows the hull to plane at top speed. It means you can sail effortlessly fast without needing to fight for control.

Watch your trim! Heeling to leeward will make the boat head up on the wave. Keep the boat flat for maximum control and bear away when a gust hits.

Racing with waves

Clever use of waves will maximise downwind speed. The object is to encourage your boat to surf with each wave. As you reach the top of a wave and start to tip down the face, trim body weight forward while pumping the sheets to promote surfing.

A Once the boat is surfing, the apparent wind will change, letting you bear away and sail deeper downwind.

B Surfing across the wave face will not only boost your speed, but also provide a more direct course to the leeward mark. Do not let the bows plough into the back of the next wave. Luff or bear away to hit the wave at an angle, trimming weight back to ensure the bows can lift with the wave instead of diving and stopping the boat.

C Turn weight forward as the wave passes.

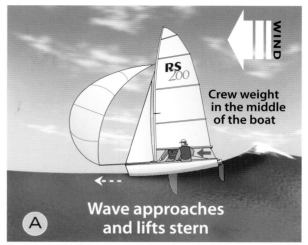

A **Wave approaches and lifts stern**

Crew weight in the middle of the boat

Catch a wave to lift the transom and accelerate the boat on a fast downhill ride.

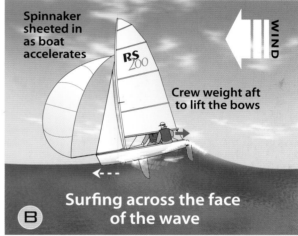

Spinnaker sheeted in as boat accelerates

Crew weight aft to lift the bows

B **Surfing across the face of the wave**

Heel the boat slightly to windward to bear away on the face of the wave, without using the rudder to steer the boat. Sheet in as apparent wind increases with boat speed.

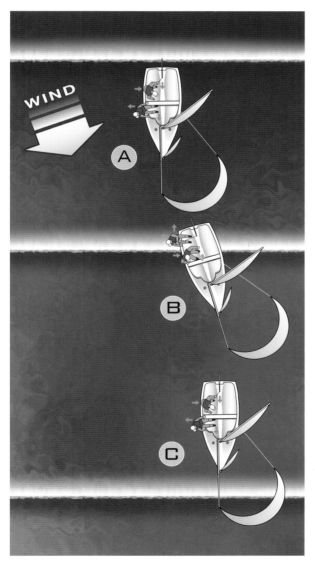

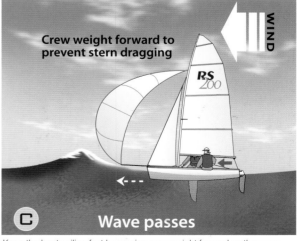

Crew weight forward to prevent stern dragging

C **Wave passes**

Keep the boat sailing fast by moving crew weight forward as the wave passes, ready to hitch a ride on the next wave. Head up by heeling slightly to leeward to prevent the bows digging into the back of the wave.

Shifts and gybes

- Unless you are on the lay line a shift to the left will favour boats on the left and vice versa - tack on the header and cross the fleet.

- Progress towards the leeward mark is the best indicator when to gybe. A dinghy with an asymmetric spinnaker can gybe without losing much speed, encouraging gybes on wind shifts in order to sail a shorter course to the leeward mark.

- A fully powered dinghy with an asymmetric spinnaker can only sail within a limited wind angle. A few degrees too low and it will slow right down; a few degrees too high and it may capsize. This is a particular issue when crossing gybes with other dinghies at high speed. Port must give way to starboard – if you have to give way, it may be preferable to gybe out of trouble.

Do not collide

When reaching downwind with an asymmetric spinnaker or running directly downwind with a symmetrical spinnaker, beware of boats sailing upwind on the windward leg. You may be sailing very fast with limited ability to manoeuvre; the spray and sails may blanket your view. Sailing downwind, you only have right of way if you are on starboard and the boat sailing upwind is on port.

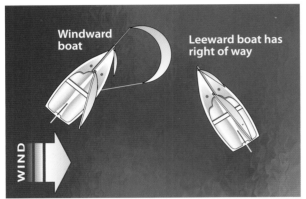

Both boats are on port tack, but the leeward boat which is sailing closer to the wind has right of way.

Beware of starboard tack boats coming up the course, when your view is obstructed by the spinnaker.

Sail light

A light boat is a fast boat. Make sure there is no water in the cockpit when sailing offwind. Push down the self-bailers or if necessary bail by hand.

Eyes in the back of your head

- When running directly downwind, be aware of boats following close behind. The problem is that they will get the next gust of wind first, which will become turbulent with less power by the time it hits your sails.

- If an identical boat is directly behind and being sailed well, it will keep closing the gap until it is right on your transom. To avoid this, sail to one side (windward) or the other (leeward) and keep watching your back!

- Sailing downwind, it may not be obvious if you are being affected by dirty wind. Look at the Windex or burgee of boats close behind. If their wind indicators are pointing straight at you, your sails will be in dirty wind. You will need to head up or gybe to escape this kind of cover.

Capsize

If you capsize with the spinnaker hoisted, pull it back into its chute or bag before attempting to right the boat. Unless the wind is very light, the boat will be blown flat with the spinnaker still hoisted, which will most likely tie itself in some interesting knots.

Capsizing with the spinnaker will lose a lot of places. The crew must pull the spinnaker back into its chute before they can right the boat.

Reaching from mark to mark

If the course has a direct single tack reach between two marks:

• Keep in the strongest wind pressure by sailing low in gusts and sailing high in lulls to maximise boat speed, but always remember that the direct rhumb line is the shortest route to the next mark.

• Sailing high and fast will take you to windward of other boats, so you are not affected by their wind shadow. However, you will have to bear away (and slow down) to reach the mark. Sailing lower and slower will take you to leeward of other boats, but you may be able to head up, accelerate and get inside them before entering the two boat length zone at the gybe mark.

• There is a natural tendency to sail too high between offwind marks on a reach, so you follow a great circle route and end up having to bear away (and slow down) to reach the mark. Sailing along the rhumb line, the mark will always appear to be to windward of your bows – unless you are sitting right in the middle of the boat!

When can you luff?

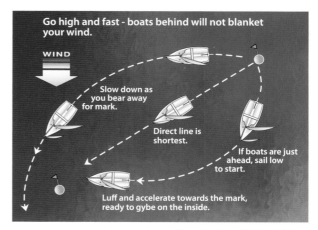

Even without waves, it is impossible to sail a perfectly straight line to the next mark. Sitting up on the windward deck, there is a natural tendency to steer high and follow a 'great circle route' on the windward side of the rhumb line. The advantage of sailing high is that you can overtake boats to leeward, through sailing faster in clear wind. However, the boat will lose speed if you have to bear away deep on the final approach to the mark, where it will be on the outside of boats approaching at full bore from the leeward side of the rhumb line.

• If a boat is overtaking on the windward side, you may not luff above your proper course (direct to the next mark) while an overlap exists. You are not permitted to luff violently forcing the other boat to change course.

• The overtaking boat must keep clear to windward, until it is clear ahead with a straight line drawn across its transom ahead of your spinnaker pole or bows.

Sailing on a tight reach, you can only luff so far without the spinnaker collapsing. Overtaking boats must keep clear.

Fast traffic at the wing mark

The wing mark at the side of the course requires a gybing transition from reach to reach. If the breeze is up, boats will be sailing very fast on a broad reach. Remember who has right of way. If a boat has an inside overlap before entering the two boat length zone, it must be given room round the mark – a boat on the outside must wait for the inside boat to gybe. If there is no overlap when a boat enters the zone, a boat on the inside must go round the mark behind the outer boat.

470s gybe from starboard to port tack at the wing mark. The next turn will be at the bottom of the course.

Gybing from a broad reach to a close reach at the wing mark. Try to get the windward slot when you gybe round the mark.

Golden Rules of Running Downwind

Leading dinghy racing coach and sailmaker Michael McNamara passes on his training tips for racing directly down a run…

"Running downwind and getting to that leeward mark as quickly as possible depends upon the inter relationship between BOAT SPEED, STRATEGY and TACTICS. Boat speed, which is simply going as fast as possible irrespective of whatever else is happening, should dominate. But the other two aspects may compete for priority, depending on circumstance."

Boat Speed

1. Boom should be eased out as far as possible and be touching the shroud to give maximum-presented sail area.

2. Use just enough kicker to keep the leech mobile with up to 75mm of forwards movement in the gusts.

3. To get maximum projected area, the soft lens foot panel should be just tight with one horizontal ridge along the boom.

4. The spinnaker should be pulled as far round to windward as possible. Remember that it is not only working in wind which is coming from astern, but is also using the accelerating air coming off the front of the mainsail.

5. The crew should be telling the helm how much load there is in the spinnaker sheet and guy. As soon as pressure eases the helm will have to luff up, but if the sail is pulling well then the helm can bear away.

6. Check that the hull is making as little resistance as possible by:

   a) The helm easing his grip on the tiller extension from time to time – if the tiller moves one way or the other, flow is not equalised. Change the angle of heel either to leeward or to windward until the tiller stays down the centreline.

   b) By looking aft at the wash, the sailors can change their positioning in the boat to minimise turbulence coming off the transom. This is especially important if the helm is sitting to leeward, because it is all too easy to sit back and heel the boat.

Strategy – using the environment to best advantage

1. It does not pay to tack downwind in displacement dinghies, because the hull cannot be made to go fast enough to make up for the extra distance sailed. However it is very hard to run exactly at 180 degrees with any accuracy. The optimum angle is likely to be when the wind is coming from the windward corner of the transom.

2. As sailing the minimum distance is so important, constantly ask the question "Is my bow pointing closer to the mark on this gybe or would it be closer on the other gybe?" The crew must know where the leeward mark is at all times.

3. The previous beat will have given clues on wind variations and strength, which can be used on the run. For example, if the boat has been mostly on starboard tack up the beat then it will go down the run mostly on port tack.

4. In a shifting wind stay away from the lay lines.

5. If the leeward mark is not exactly 180 degrees downwind, take the longest leg first as there is less chance of over standing the mark.

6. The approach to the windward mark can help decide which gybe to go on first. If the boat is being headed into the mark, the boat should start the run on the same gybe. If the boat is being freed into the mark, the boat should start the run by gybing.

Overtaking a fleet of much slower Optimists provides an additional tactical challenge for these Cadet sailors.

Tactics – against other boats

1. The aim in boat-to-boat tactics is to maximise the detrimental effect of your boat on the opposition, whilst minimising their detrimental effect on yourself.

2. Boats behind have the advantage, as they will be able to cover boats in front. To find out whether a boat is being covered, look at the wind indicator of the covering boat. If it is pointing at the boat in front and they are within about 10 boat lengths, then you can be sure that boat is covered.

3. Boats that are being covered should move urgently one way or the other, until the indicator of the covering boat is not pointing in their direction.

4. Boats grouped together will be sailing slower in less wind than boats by themselves, because they present a barrier to the wind which lifts off the water long before it gets to them.

5. Use the last quarter of the run to organise being on the inside at the leeward mark.

You're never alone on the race course – watch out for the guys coming from behind with the purple spinnaker!

14 | Bottom of the Course

The race may finish near the leeward mark at the bottom of the course, or continue with another beat all the way up the course to the windward mark...

RS800 makes its final approach to the leeward mark on Lake Garda. Remember the golden rule – 'in wide, out tight.'

- Go in wide and come out as tight as possible at the leeward mark. This ensures you can start the upwind leg in the best possible position, pointing high and sailing fast, with no boat to windward.

- Turn the boat upwind as fast as you can pull in the mainsheet, to pull on more power. Letting the boat heel to windward will help turn it towards the wind, but don't heel too far or the boat will slip sideways and slow down.

- If you are stuck immediately behind a boat when you turn upwind, you must tack to break cover without delay. Watch out for boats which are still sailing downwind to the leeward mark. You cannot tack in their path, but will have right of way as soon as you are sailing on starboard tack.

Approaching with the bow a metre off the mark leaves space to…

…turn the whole boat right next to the mark…

…and depart with maximum windward advantage.

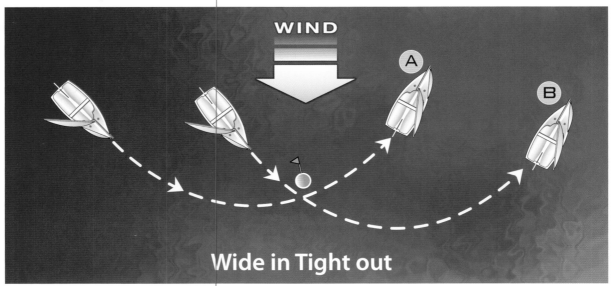

WIND

Wide in Tight out

B goes in tight and comes out wide. A goes in wide and comes out tight, starting the beat with a windward position advantage.

Top Tip

When turning upwind from a run or a reach, use both hands to sheet in the mainsail. Pulling in hand-over-hand is twice as quick and much more effective than using one hand to pull the sheet through the jamming cleat.

1. Pull in with your front hand, drawing it towards your back hand which is holding the tiller extension in the normal dagger (downward grasp) position.

2. Transfer the taut sheet to your back hand which will lock the sheet in that position, as you reach forward with the front hand to grab more sheet.

3. Keep pulling in, transferring between front hand and back hand, with a steady rhythm.

What is the tide doing?

- If the tide is flowing against you, as you approach the leeward mark, you can leave the spinnaker drop or pushing down the daggerboard until the last moment, since the approach will be comparatively slow.

- If the tide is flowing with you, it may be necessary to drop the spinnaker or push down the daggerboard well ahead of time. It's not good to start the beat with the spinnaker hoisted or the daggerboard half up – you will look silly and go sideways!

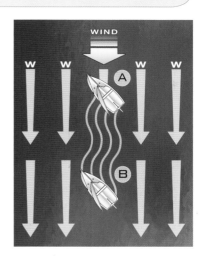

Consolidate your position by covering. The object is to ensure that boats directly behind sail in the same wind and cannot get an advantage elsewhere on the course.

Another beat to the windward mark

- The number of laps and format of the race will have been indicated by the committee boat at the start.

- Boats are likely to be more spread out on the second windward leg than on the first, so you will not have to deal with the crowded conditions in the early stages after the start.

- If you round the windward mark and start sailing upwind on port tack, keep a look out for boats still sailing downwind on starboard tack.

- If the priority is to consolidate your position by not letting other boats overtake, keep sailing between them and the finish line. Boats to leeward and behind will be stuck in your dirty wind, and will not be able to overtake unless they can break this cover. Nor will they be able to benefit from different wind conditions on other parts of the course. The downside of this tactic is that boats which you are chasing may get even further ahead, due to picking more favourable wind shifts.

15 At the End of the Race

All you have to do is cross the line to finish, then wait for the next race to start if racing is being held 'back-to-back.' If it's the end of racing for the day, be sure to sign off before derigging your boat. This will confirm that you have complied with the rules and are safely ashore...

Finish

- Most races finish with an upwind leg, allowing boats to cross a finish line, which should be laid at right angles to the wind so neither end is favoured. However, the line will almost certainly be slightly skewed, with one end slightly downwind (to leeward). That end will be closest, so go for it! For safety, cross the nearest end of the finish line on starboard tack, unless there are no other boats to contend with.

- If you sail beyond the lay line for the finish and there is a boat to leeward, you are allowed to call for room to cross the finish line, despite being the windward boat.

- The finish may be offwind at the bottom of the course, either coming in on a broad reach from the side or gybing downwind from the windward mark with an asymmetric spinnaker. If it is a single tack reaching finish, protect your windward side and remember the restrictions on luffing rights. If it is a gybe-to-gybe downwind finish, it's likely to be much safer to finish on starboard tack sailing at full bore with a kite!

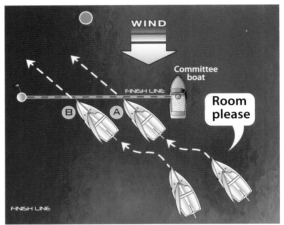

A is upwind of the finish line, but is permitted to ask B for room to bear away and cross the line, despite being windward boat.

- Make sure the finish boat has logged your finish. If you expect a 'gun' (sound signal) and don't get one, it will almost certainly mean you have been disqualified (DSQ) for being over the start line and not returning. What a waste of a race!

Back on the shore

- Post a tally or sign off as required at the end of racing.

- Discuss and analyse the race.

- Fix anything on the boat that needs changing. Check that all the sail controls still work.

"That's it! Well done!"

Race Scoring

The team with the lowest number of points wins a race series overall. Races are scored as follows:

1st place: 1 point.

2nd place: 2 points.

3rd place: 3 points, etc.

DNS/DNC (did not start/did not compete) counts total number of starters plus 1.

PMS (premature start) counts total number of starters plus 2.

DSQ (disqualified) counts total number of starters plus 1.

RET (retired) counts total number of starters plus 1.

Competitors are generally allowed one or two discards in a race series, allowing them not to count their worst results.

Penalties & Protests

• A collision or hitting a mark is a rule infringement. The rule-breaking crew can *'take a penalty by promptly making one complete 360° turn including one tack and one gybe'* which should exonerate them. Alternatively, a 720 which is two 360s may be required. Find out what penalties are in place before the race.

• If another boat breaks a rule but does not do penalty turns, then you may protest. Inform the other boat that you intend to protest by calling "Protest." If they still do not take a penalty, you should inform the race officer of your protest at the end of the race and complete a race protest form. The Protest Committee adjudicates. If found guilty, the rule-breaker is DSQ.

• Protests are rare and can lead to bad feeling in a sporting event. Best advice is to avoid them if at all possible!

"Yeah, wicked!" There will be tales to tell at the end of a long, hard race!

Waiting for the prizes at the Topper World Championship.

16 Keep Out of Trouble

Things that go wrong might include:

1. Failing to check that your boat is set up correctly before the race. For instance it's embarrassing to hoist a spinnaker and discover it's sheeted inside the forestay, or start filling with water because an inspection hatch is not tightly closed.

2. Starting the race a few seconds late, so you're sailing with boats immediately to windward, leeward or ahead, all of which are creating dirty turbulent wind. The situation could be even worse if you started at the wrong end of the line.

3. Getting pushed over the line, by boats to leeward or the tide, before the start. So you need to go back and recross the line, without obstructing other boats.

4. Hitting the committee boat or getting trapped by its anchor line. Very embarrassing!

5. Once you have left the start line, failing to tack as soon as possible to clear your wind.

6. Choosing the wrong side of the course with less wind and an adverse tide.

7. Failing to react to a heading wind shift, which forces you to bear away and point further from the windward mark. Then failing to react when the wind shifts again. How you react to wind shifts will to a large extent depend on the boat you are sailing. If the boat tacks quickly, you can can spin round on every advantageous shift. If the boat tacks slowly but can sail very fast to windward – as with a skiff – you may lose out by tacking unless there is a major wind shift.

8. Overstanding the lay line, so you have to bear away and sail down to the windward mark where you must give way to boats approaching on the leeward side. This problem is often caused by not allowing for tide.

9. Tacking too early for the mark, and then trying to pinch in order to squeeze round. The normal result is that you will be getting rolled by a stream of boats on the windward side. The only way out of this mess is to wait for a gap to windward and tack back onto port. This problem could

be caused by the tide, but may also be caused by tacking too early in light winds when it is impossible to power up to the mark. This becomes a major problem when a stream of boats are creating a large area of dirty wind. If it looks crowded, always tack late.

10. Failing to give way round the mark, when the same-tack boat on the inside established an overlap before it was three boat lengths from the mark. You have to take a penalty turn, without obstructing other boats. You would also have to take a penalty if you try to barge round the inside at the last moment.

11. Appoaching a port hand (leave to port) mark on port tack is very high risk when boats are approaching on starboard tack. If you obstruct a starboard tack boat while tacking to go round the mark, a penalty will be required.

12. Colliding with or obstructing a competitor, who is still sailing upwind on either tack as you start sailing downwind on port tack. This can easily happen in the excitement of bearing away, changing sail controls and accelerating offwind, particularly if the helm's view is obstructed by the spinnaker. Once again, you will have to take a penalty.

13. Sailing too far off to the windward side on a single-tack reaching leg to the wing mark. Apart from sailing further than boats on the direct rhumb line, you have to bear away and consequently slow down on the final approach to the mark. You then arrive on the outside, and have to give way to boats approaching on the rhumb line or shooting up at high speed from leeward.

14. Bearing down on a leeward boat and obstructing its course. Once again you have to take a penalty.

15. Pushing the boat too hard and taking risks in stronger winds. A lot of time can be lost getting back into the race after a capsize.

16. Turning round the leeward mark with the spinnaker still half hoisted and the centreboard or daggerboard only half down. Apart from looking silly, your boat will get blown sideways instead of powering upwind.

17. Failing to go in wide and come out tight at the leeward mark, so any boats on the inside will start giving you dirty wind.

18. Forgetting to cover boats coming up behind on the last windward leg, so they find a part of the course with better wind and slip ahead before the finish.

19. Crossing the windward (furthest) instead of the leeward (nearest) end of the finish line.

20. Forgetting to sign off or post a tally to confirm you have finished the race and are safely ashore.

"Whatever you do, don't fall over!"

Dave Evans and Rick Peacock look for a way out during a 49er race at the World Sailing Championships in Cascais

17 | Trim for Speed

If you want to win a race, the first requirement is to finish, the second is to sail consistently faster than any other boat, and the third is to make the least mistakes all the way round the course...

470 crew Joe Glanfield stays flat out on the trapeze as helm Nick Rogers tidies a spinnaker sheet

17 | Trim for Speed

Keeping a boat sailing at full speed requires a combination of skill and concentration, relying on fundamental use of sail and boat trim to ensure optimum speed…

Trim is fundamental

- Sail trim and boat trim are the two main ingredients required to sail a boat at the fastest possible speed. The best way to get a perfect understanding of trim is to try sailing without a rudder. With practice you should be able to beat, reach, run, tack and gybe by simply moving body weight and trimming the sheets. Pull the rudder blade clear of the water for this exercise. The boat will be more responsive if you partly lift the centreboard or daggerboard, reducing the heeling and turning forces of the foil.

- If the boat heels to leeward, it will want to turn into the wind. Pulling in the mainsheet (powering up) has the same effect of turning the boat into the wind, due to loading up the centre of effort which is behind the centre of lateral resistance, represented by the foil. Heeling and sheeting can be used together to steer the boat.

- If the boat heels to windward, it will tend to steer away from the wind. Letting out the mainsheet (depowering) and pulling in the jib (powering up) will have the same effect. Heeling and sheeting can be used together.

- If the boat heels to leeward, it will be difficult to steer away from the wind. If the boat heels to windward, it will be difficult to steer towards the wind.

- The rudder helps steer the boat and provides fine-tuning, but must be used in conjunction with sail and boat trim for maximum effectiveness. The rudder will be least effective at high sailing speeds, when sail and boat trim should dictate where the boat goes. Over use of the rudder will provide a brake on the transom, which slows the boat down.

"OMG!" These guys are having a spot of bother.

Don't drag the stern

- The boat must be correctly trimmed fore and aft. Sailing upwind in light or moderate winds, it is normal to shift crew weight as far forward as possible – in a class such as the RS200, the crew would be right next to the windward shroud. This helps lift the transom to prevent it dragging and slowing the boat down. It also pushes down the bows, which will increase waterline length for a slight boost in performance.

- As boat speed increases, the stern will lift and the bows will start to get pushed down. The crew must move their weight aft to let the bows skim the water, without burying and dragging the stern. Depending on the type of boat and conditions, constant fore and aft movement may be required to ensure optimum trim. Sailing by the seat of the pants is the best way to assess how the boat is performing, but requires a backlog of experience.

Time to shift weight forward to keep moving with that wave.

Keep the boat upright

All modern dinghies are designed to be sailed as upright as possible. If you let a dinghy heel too far to leeward, it will:

1. Slip sideways, due to less resistance from the centreboard or daggerboard.

2. Lose power, due to less pressure driving the sails.

3. Slow down, due to the side of the hull burying in the water.

4. Be difficult to steer, due to a natural tendency to turn into the wind (weather helm). This will be even more difficult to control if the rudder blade is partly lifted out of the water.

The solution is to keep the dinghy flat by hiking out harder, easing out the mainsheet or luffing into the wind during gusts. If the rig is permanently overpowered, the mainsail must be depowered by tensioning the Cunningham and kicking strap. This will move the centre of effort forward and twist open the top of the sail, allow airflow to escape without powering up the rig. On a double-handed boat, airflow between the mainsail and jib can be reduced by using the barber hauler to move the jib sheet outboard, which will widen the slot between the sails. If necessary, part-lift the centreboard or daggerboard to reduce heeling moment.

Use whatever hiking style suits, but stay upright.

How to use telltales

- Wind streams over both sides of a sail, creating high pressure on the windward side and low pressure on the leeward side. This pressure pulls and sucks the sail, while the shape of the hull and the foils ensure sail power will drive the boat ahead.

- Telltales are lightweight streamers – sometimes known as woolies – which are attached at different heights near the leading edge of the jib or mainsail. Telltales provide information on how wind is flowing across the sails. Sailing upwind, the windward telltales should be starting to stream slightly upwards, while the leeward telltales stream back horizontally.

- Telltales are only effective when there is airflow on both sides of the sail. They provide little information when running downwind.

- If all the windward telltales stop streaming, you either need to pull in the sheet or bear away. If all the leeward telltales stop streaming, you either need to ease out the sheet or head up. Windward telltales provide instant feedback when sailing upwind or on a reach; leeward telltales will be slower to respond to changes in wind flow.

- There are normally two or three sets of telltales at different heights on the sail. They will not all stream perfectly in unison. Owing to sail twist (the leech of the sail is more open at the top), upper telltales may start to lift while lower telltales still stream aft. It is the lower telltales that matter most, providing feedback on the area where maximum power is generated.

- The jib can be tricky to trim precisely when sailing on a reach. To find the range in which you need to trim the jib, pull in the sheet until the windward telltale collapses, and then ease the sheet until the leeward telltale collapses. Note that the upper telltales will collapse first.

- Beware that a wet telltale may stick to the sail and provide inaccurate feedback.

The leeward telltale on Paul Goodison's Laser is absolutely horizontal, indicating perfect trim.

UNDER-TRIMMING	CORRECT TRIM	OVER-TRIMMING

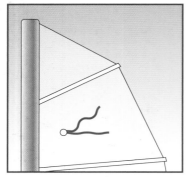

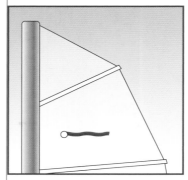

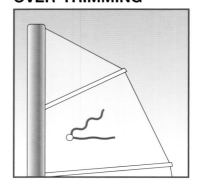

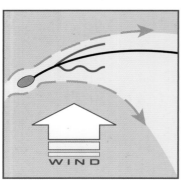

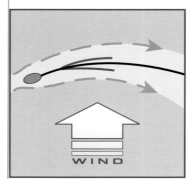

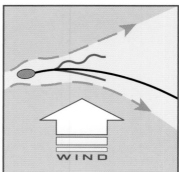

PULL IN THE SHEET OR BEAR AWAY

LET OUT THE SHEET OR HEAD UP

29ers race at the Youth National Championships. Being able to see both sides of the Mylar© sails makes the use of telltales doubly effective.

18 | Make the Most of the Wind

The wind is the vital ingredient which drives your boat round the course. Make sure you use it to maximum benefit…

Sailing directly downwind demands intense concentration.
Perfect trim helps provide maximum speed on waves.

How close can you sail upwind?

- Use intuition and feel to match your course to the wind.

- Watch gusts blowing across the water towards the windward side of the bows. Be ready to respond by hiking hard or easing the mainsheet.

- Watch the windward telltales to steer the boat as close to the wind as possible, ensuring there is clean airflow across the sails. This will allow you to power upwind, without needing to constantly trim the mainsheet, saving your arm muscles and leaving you free to concentrate on steering the best course.

- If you bear away from the optimum upwind course, the sails will begin to generate more power. The result is that the boat will heel over, unless you ease the mainsheet.

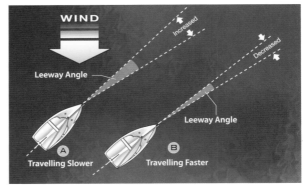

A is pointing higher but sailing slower than B, which will make less leeway thanks to increased lift.

Despite a flat pram bow, the Cadet points high with a sophisticated modern rig.

Bear away a few degrees for a big increase in speed.

Mast rake

- The mast should be upright to provide maximum power in lighter winds, but may need to be raked slightly aft to promote pointing. If the mast is raked too far aft, it will create weather helm which may make the boat difficult to steer.

- Raking the mast aft moves the Centre of Effort (main fulcrum of power in the sails) further behind the Centre of Lateral Resistance (where the boat would turn about the centreboard or daggerboard). It also has the effect of lowering the Centre of Effort, making the boat easier to control in stronger wind and enabling it to point higher while beating.

- Dinghies without shrouds, such as the Laser, have a fixed position mast that cannot be raked fore or aft.

- Dinghies such as the RS200 provide mast rake adjustment in the boat park. This is achieved by changing jib luff tension and changing the length of the shrouds with different pin positions on the shroud plates.

- Dinghies such as the Merlin Rocket have highly refined and complex rig control systems, which allow the rig to be raked fore and aft while the boat is racing. This would normally be used to depower the rig by raking the mast aft when sailing upwind, and to repower the rig for raking the mast back upright for sailing downwind.

Apparent wind

- True wind is wind direction and speed blowing onto a fixed object, such as a sailing club anemometer.

- Apparent wind is wind direction and speed blowing onto a moving object. If a boat is sailing at a speed of 5 knots towards a true wind of 10 knots, the apparent wind experienced by the crew and flowing over the sails will be close to 15 knots. If a boat is sailing at a speed of 5 knots away from a true wind of 10 knots, the apparent wind experienced by the crew and flowing over the sails will be close to 5 knots. That helps explain why it often seems to be colder and windier beating upwind than sailing downwind.

- The speed of the boat through the water alters the angle of the apparent wind. As the boat accelerates, the apparent wind swings forward so it is blowing from further ahead. This phenomenon is most obvious on windsurfers, catamarans and skiff-style dinghies, which always appear to have their sails sheeted in tight when there is a good breeze. High boat speed ensures that the apparent wind angle swings onto the bows, even though they may be sailing downwind. When sailing a skiff, the crew will always want to boost the apparent wind.

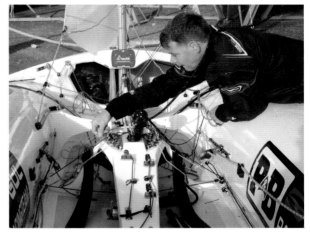

The adjustable strut helps control mast rake and mast bend, combined with fully adjustable shrouds on a 505. The whole rig can be moved fore and aft with a quick pull on a control line, without losing speed during a race. Ian Pinnell (below) shows the complex mass of control lines in the cockpit.

Apparent wind speed boosts your power for maximum performance offwind. Ian Pinnell (505 world champion in 2008) teamed up with Ian Mitchell (505 world champion in 1997 and 2006) for this high speed test session.

Go for speed or height?

- Many classic dinghies are optimised when sailing quite slowly to windward, but pointing very high towards the wind. However, if waves are hitting the bows and slowing the boat, it will pay to bear off slightly and go for more speed. Move crew weight slightly aft to help lift the bows, particularly in stronger winds.

- Skiff-style dinghies – typically with a lightweight, flat-bottomed hull powered by an oversize rig – are designed to plane upwind in a moderate breeze. If you attempt to point high, the boat will stall and slow right down. You must sail the boat free and fast upwind for maximum VMG (velocity made good), while also holding it as flat as possible on the water by hiking or trapezing.

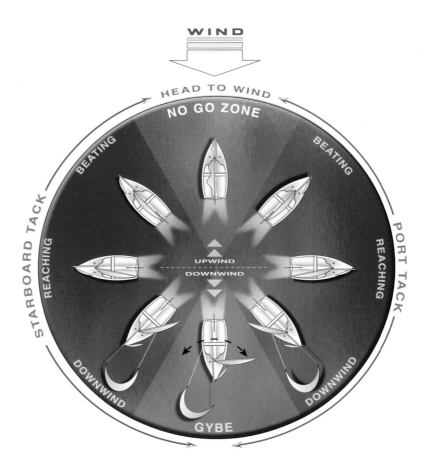

Use a compass

Digital or glass ball compasses can give a tactical advantage. A racing compass will make it easier to spot and react to wind shifts. It will provide comparative headings on port and starboard tack, when tacking upwind or gybing downwind, making it much easier to judge the lay ine to the next mark. It can also be used to evaluate line bias before the start, and if racing on a large course may be vital to provide headings to marks which are almost out of sight. Top spec instruments combine a digital compass with a digital race timer, providing immediate information all the way round the course.

Standard scale 0-360

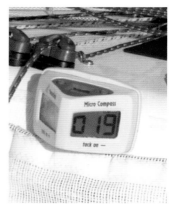
Digital Micro Compass.

- To check line bias, sail from the starboard end of the line (this ensures you are on starboad tack) directly towards the port end of the line and take a bearing on where the bows are pointing. If the angle is 90 degrees, the line is square. If the line is less than 90 degrees, the port end is favoured. If the line is more than 90 degrees, the starboard end is favoured. A difference of 5 degrees will make little difference; a difference of 20 degrees will make it critical to start from the favoured end.

- When racing upwind, the numbers show your bearing. If the numbers rise on starboard tack, you are being lifted closer to the windward mark. If the numbers decrease, you are being headed and should tack. On port tack you are being lifted when the numbers decrease, and lifted when the numbers increase.

- The difference between headers and lifters will provide a mean course for each tack. This can help decide whether you will be lifted or headed on rounding the leeward mark at the bottom of the course, and should stay on the same tack or tack off in the other direction.

Sailing to windward at full speed in 30 knots true wind! It's possible with great technique and sophisticated control systems.

Windward leg wind watch

Once you are fully hiked out over the side or on the trapeze, the only variables while sailing upwind will be trimming the mainsheet and steering with the tiller, with the jib sheet correctly cleated for the wind strength. The helm concentrates on steering through waves, while adjusting the mainsheet to hold the boat upright during gusts. The crew looks ahead to spot gusts and wind shifts, providing information for the helm; at the same time the crew must watch other boats, in order to forestall right of way problems or difficulties with dirty wind. Some classes and especially top crews do play the jib particularly in big gusts. This stops the slot getting closed when the mainsail is eased out.

Sheets are the primary tools used to control the angle of attack of mainsail and jib. Secondary rig controls help govern the shape and amount of power in the sails, as you race round the course…

Ian Pinnell and Ian Mitchell power upwind in 30 knots. Note the wide slot between the jib and mainsail, which points directly into the wind, with only a small amount of centreboard to lift the boat to windward.

19 Rig Controls

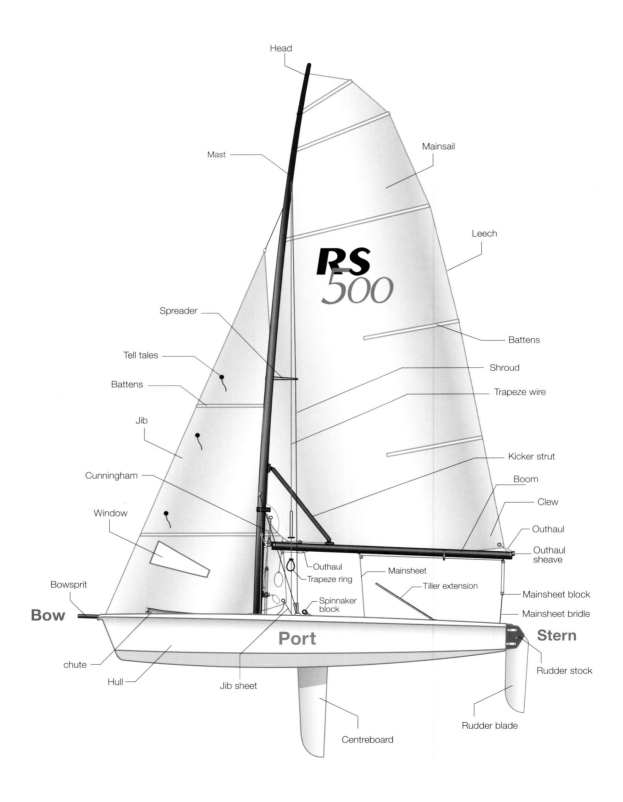

Head

Mast

Mainsail

Leech

Spreader

Tell tales

Battens

Battens

Jib

Shroud

Trapeze wire

Cunningham

Kicker strut

Boom

Clew

Window

Outhaul

Outhaul
sheave

Outhaul

Trapeze ring

Mainsheet

Tiller extension

Mainsheet block

Mainsheet bridle

Bowsprit

Spinnaker
block

Bow

Port

Stern

chute

Rudder stock

Hull

Jib sheet

Rudder blade

Centreboard

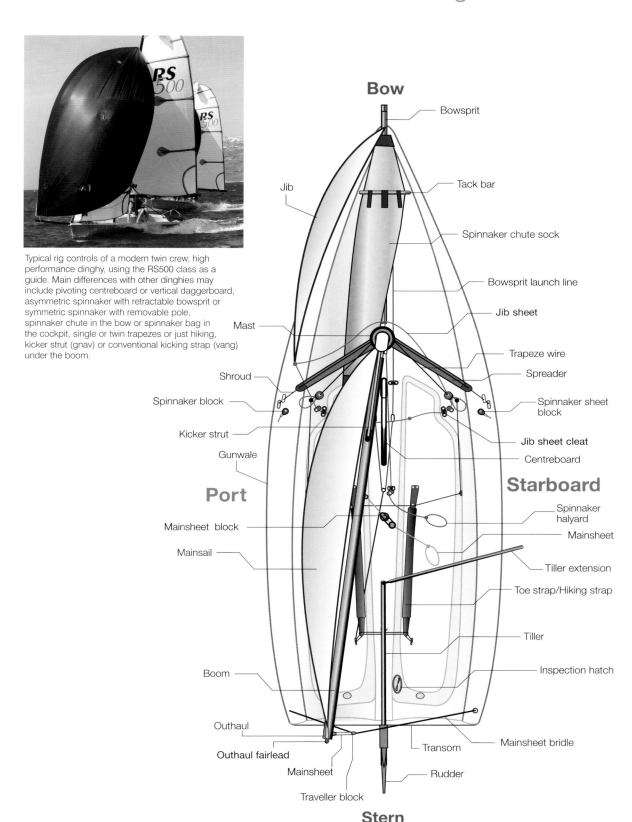

Typical rig controls of a modern twin crew, high performance dinghy, using the RS500 class as a guide. Main differences with other dinghies may include pivoting centreboard or vertical daggerboard, asymmetric spinnaker with retractable bowsprit or symmetric spinnaker with removable pole, spinnaker chute in the bow or spinnaker bag in the cockpit, single or twin trapezes or just hiking, kicker strut (gnav) or conventional kicking strap (vang) under the boom.

Bow

Bowsprit

Tack bar

Spinnaker chute sock

Bowsprit launch line

Jib sheet

Trapeze wire

Spreader

Spinnaker sheet block

Jib sheet cleat

Centreboard

Starboard

Spinnaker halyard

Mainsheet

Tiller extension

Toe strap/Hiking strap

Tiller

Inspection hatch

Mainsheet bridle

Transom

Rudder

Stern

Jib

Mast

Shroud

Spinnaker block

Kicker strut

Gunwale

Port

Mainsheet block

Mainsail

Boom

Outhaul

Outhaul fairlead

Mainsheet

Traveller block

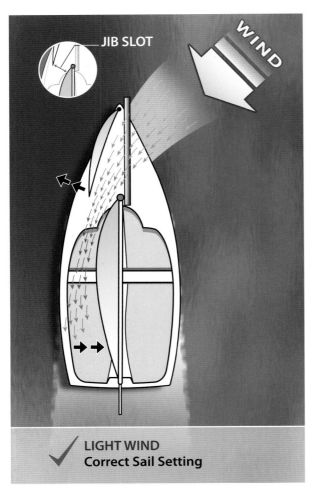

JIB SLOT

WIND

✓ **LIGHT WIND**
Correct Sail Setting

A tight jib slot provides maximum power, thanks to accelerated airflow over the leeward side of the mainsail.

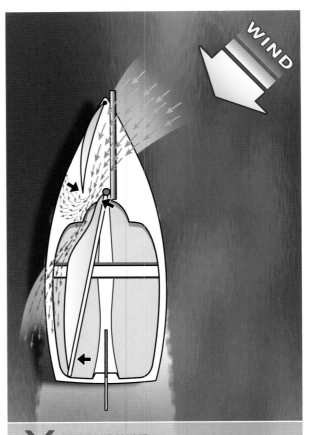

WIND

✗ **STRONG WIND**
Incorrect Sail Setting

Easing the mainsheet will not solve the problem if you have too much power in stronger winds. The slot between jib and mainsail must be wide enough to allow clean airflow.

Jib controls

- Jib sheets are used to adjust the horizontal angle of the jib, to ensure it has the optimum 'angle of attack' to the wind. However, when the jib sheet is eased, the clew of the sail will tend to lift vertically.

- A jib car changes the vertical angle of each sheet. Move the car forward to tighten the leech and increase power in the top of the jib when sailing offwind; move the car back to open the leech and decrease power in the top of the jib when sailing upwind.

- A barber-hauler changes the position of each jib sheet fairlead. Move the barber hauler inboard to close the slot between jib and mainsail, accelerating airflow to increase power in lighter winds. Move the barber-hauler outboard to open the slot, decelerating airflow to decrease power in stronger winds.

> ### Top Tip
> Always wear sailing gloves with reinforced palms. You will be able to pull a lot harder and longer on control lines and sheets!

Mainsheet

- The mainsheet controls the horizontal angle of the mainsail, which is like a curved foil with wind flow divided over its windward and leeward surfaces.

- Virtually all modern dinghies have a centre mainsheet, with a sheet lead from the centre of the cockpit. Transom mainsheets were standard on most dinghies until the 1970s, when centre mainsheets began to take over.

- Pulling in the mainsheet tight will increase leech tension in light winds. The mainsheet should be hand-held as much as possible, to enable the helm to sheet in and out during gusts. This is necessary to prevent the dinghy heeling to leeward (gust) or windward (lull) while sailing a straight course. Most dinghies are fitted with an auto-ratchet block, which can be set to on (you can hear the clicks as it locks) or off (free running for faster response, but harder to hold).

- On some classes, such as the 29er, the mainsheet is led from the middle of the boom to enable the crew to trim the mainsail upwind. This allows the helm to concentrate on steering the boat, while the crew can use both hands to trim the mainsheet from a powerful pulling position on the trapeze. Other classes, such as the RS800, do not allow the crew to trim the mainsheet, believing that this technique may be too demanding for mixed crews who want to enjoy racing without needing high levels of muscle or expertise.

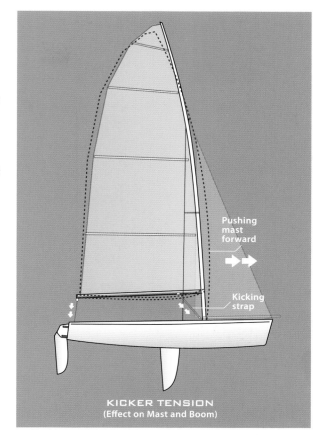

Pushing mast forward

Kicking strap

KICKER TENSION
(Effect on Mast and Boom)

Andy Davis of Speed Sails charges upwind in his Merlin Rocket in Force 4. You can see how the Cunningham pulls down the luff of the mainsail, which compresses the mast. The aluminium 'horse' in the middle of the cockpit allows precise control of boom angle.

Kicking Strap

The kicking strap or 'kicker' (also know as a 'boom vang' in America) holds down the boom. It is used to maintain sail twist, bending the mast and tensioning the leech. A gnav (vang spelt backwards) is a strut on top of the boom which provides an inverted kicking strap. Its main advantage is to free up space in the cockpit directly behind the mast. The kicking strap is mainly used in moderate to strong winds. If you are overpowered, increase kicking strap tension; if you are underpowered, decrease kicking strap tension.

Conventional kicking strap or vang on Laser 2000.

Gnav or boom strut on RS500.

Cunningham

The Cunningham (invented by Briggs Cunningham) or downhaul is a multi-purchase control line used to tension the luff of the mainsail. This compresses the mast which therefore bends and pulls the mainsail forward. The effect is to move the centre of effort forwards and open the top half of the leech, which is highly effective at depowering the mainsail in stronger winds.

Outhaul

The outhaul pulls the tack of the mainsail out along the boom and is used to control depth (also known as 'camber') which determines power in the lower part of the sail.

What is sail twist?

• A sail is not a rigid wing. Its shape is most stable along the luff where the sail is connected to the full length of the mast, and also along the foot where the sail is connected to both ends of the boom (on some dinghies, connected to the full length).

• The leech will set in a curve, known as twist. Increased twist plays an important role in depowering the mainsail in stronger winds. The top of the mainsail twists open, which means it sets like a flat blade aligned with the apparent wind. It therefore creates minimal power or heeling moment at the top of the sail.

Outhaul controls tension in the foot of the sail.

Both mainsail and jib are twisting open and getting rid of excess power, allowing the 505 to sail upwind without heeling in Force 6.

Advanced Rig Controls

Dinghies such as the Laser rely on four simple rig controls – mainsheet, kicking strap, Cunningham and outhaul – to adjust the horizontal angle of the mainsail and its shape. At the other end of the scale, some dinghies have much more refined rig controls, which allow the crew to rake the mast fore and aft, and control how it bends. Control systems will vary from class to class, but the following guidelines are typical.

Rig tension

Increased rig tension is recommended for racing in stronger winds, particularly when sailing on flat water. Rig tension should be used to keep the luff of the jib luff taut. If it sags to leeward, the boat will not be able to point. For precise measurement, use a tension gauge.

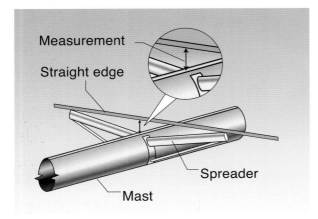

Mast rake

- Letting off the jib halyard rakes the mast back to reduce power; pulling the jib halyard on rakes the mast forward to increase power.

- Mast rake is measured from the top of the mast to the top of the transom to provide precise, comparative settings,

- When sailing upright, the boat should have just a slight feel of weather helm. If you rake the rig aft to depower the rig in stronger winds, it may be necessary to partly retract the centreboard or daggerboard to keep the boat balanced. If the rudder feels heavy, try sailing with less board down.

Dangly pole provides precise control of jib leech and foot tension

Adjustable shrouds

Mast ram or 'muscle box'

Mast bend

- A mast ram is used to limit forward bend in the bottom section of the mast. Increased bend reduces power. Different types of ram range from an adjustable 'muscle box' to simple blocks which are inserted in front of the mast when the boat is rigged.

- Main shrouds can be adjusted to bend the mast, either for pre-bend when rigging or while racing with sophisticated rig controls.

- Lower shrouds support mast bend at the bottom of the mast and can be adjusted in conjunction with mast ram.

- Raking spreaders back pre-bends the mast when rigging; raking spreaders forward reduces pre-bend. Spreader length affects sideways stiffness.

Have you got a dangly pole?

On dinghies with a mainsail and jib, but no spinnaker, a pole is used for goose winging the jib on the windward side when running downwind. A more refined option is a dangly pole which slides up and down a track on the mast, in order to increase or reduce its length. This is used to tension the leech for extra power on a reach, or when sailing downwind.

Mainsheet tracks

Full length mainsheet tracks were once very popular for racing dinghies, but are now out of favour. However, some classes have a short track which allows the sheeting position of the mainsail to be changed. In light winds, the mainsheet can be sheeted from the windward end of the track. This pulls the boom onto the centreline of the boat where it is most effective, without pulling down on the leech due to excess mainsheet tension.

Typical settings for a highly refined rig – as recommended for a National 12 where everything can be adjusted during the race.

Upwind

More power	Straighten mast by tensioning lowers or increasing mast ram.
Less power	Bend mast by releasing lowers or decreasing mast ram. Tension Cunningham. Rake mast back by easing forestay.

Downwind

More power	Straighten mast by tensioning lowers. Release Cunningham. Release outhaul. Release leeward shroud. Rake mast forward by tensioning forestay. Use dangly pole to tension jib leech.
Less power	Tension leeward shroud. Tension outhaul.

Dual controls for helm and crew on a Merlin Rocket

The National 12 provides ultra refined control of a sail 2-rig. The helmsman is Tom Stewart, sailmaker for Pinnell & Bax and multiple national champion

20 | Light Wind Performance

Racing in the Force 0-2 wind band, when there is very little breeze and no requirement to hike out, demands patience, commitment and intense concentration...

Position

- In very light winds, you may need to heel the boat slightly to leeward in order to make the sails set on the correct side. This will also provide feedback from the rudder by creating weather helm (turning to windward), which gives the tiller some 'bite'. Beware that excess weather helm will slow the boat down due to the braking effect of the rudder blade. Keep rudder movement to a minimum.

- On a single-hander you need to crouch or kneel in the cockpit; on a double-hander the crew should sit on the leeward side behind the boom.

- Keep weight well forward and avoid making any sudden movement. Try to stay still in the boat while coaxing it gently up to speed. Maximum concentration will be required. If there is any turbulence at the transom, it shows that you need to move crew weight further forward. This is particularly important on a modern skiff-style design with very flat rocker (longitudinal curve in the hull). You may need to sit uncomfortably far forward to lift the stern.

- Beware of waves – such as chop from a passing powercraft – which may stop the boat and shake the wind out of its sails. Bear away to power up the rig before you hit chop. Move crew weight to prevent the boat pitching and shaking the rig.

- Make sure the centreboard or daggerboard is fully down when sailing upwind. Retract it when sailing offwind, but not on a skiff-style dinghy where the board stays fully down.

- If the wind has almost disappeared some people recommend you try shutting your eyes to momentarily feel the wind direction.

Paul Goodison shows the level of concentration required in light winds

Steve Cockerell sits forward in the Phantom to prevent stern drag, with the boat heeled to get shape in the sail.

Sail control

- The mast should be raked upright to provide maximum power. The mainsail should be set flat to promote airflow, but without tightening the leech. If possible, the mast should be slightly bent to flatten the mainsail, for instance by raking the spreaders aft.

- Slacken off the kicking strap. This will allow the boom to lift and the mainsail to twist, enhancing wind flow over windward and leeward sides of the sail.

- Do not pull down any Cunningham tension. There may be creases in the mainsail, but they should not inhibit performance in light winds.

- Pull the outhaul tight to encourage a flat sail shape, which will increase airflow over the bottom of the mainsail.

- The boom should be pulled in to the centreline of the boat, but with the least possible downward pressure. Some dinghies have a mainsheet traveller, which makes it possible to pull the mainsheet lead from the windward side.

- If you sheet in too tightly when sailing upwind, the sails will stall. This will reduce pointing ability and speed. Ease the sheets and bear away to build power.

- Bear away until telltales are streaming on both sides of the mainsail.

- Windward jib telltales should be starting to lift, with jib sheet cars pulled back to tension the foot and twist the leech.

Even planing skiff designs like the 29er have to race in light winds!

Top Tip

- Hit the start line at full speed, to get the best chance of avoiding dirty wind.

- Look for parts of the course with the most wind. It's worth sailing a longer distance if you can find a breeze.

- Beware of tacking too early for the windward mark lay line and keep well clear of boats producing dirty wind.

1. Heel boat slightly to leeward.

2. Keep crew weight forward to lift the stern.

3. Centreboard or daggerboard fully down.

4. Straight, upright mast for maximum mainsail power.

5. Slack kicking strap allowing the mainsail to twist and 'hold' the wind.

6. No Cunningham tension. Do not worry about horizontal creases in the sail.

7. Outhaul pulled tight to end of boom.

8. Flat mainsail to increase airflow over windward and leeward sides.

9. Telltales on leech streaming.

10. Windward side telltales on jib starting to lift.

21 Moderate Wind Performance

Racing in the Force 2-4 wind band, ranging from the crew sitting on the windward side deck to fully hiked out or on the trapeze. The aim is to develop maximum power in the rig, with the boat held upright by the crew…

Position

- The boat must be kept as upright as possible, by hiking or going out on the trapeze.

- Keep crew weight forward to ensure the transom does not drag, but shift weight aft to lift the bows over waves or when the dinghy starts planing.

- Centreboard or daggerboard should be fully down for sailing upwind. Depending on the type of boat, the board may need to be part-retracted on a reach and fully retracted downwind. On skiff-style dinghies, the board generally stays fully down all the way round the course.

- Aim to sail free and fast, and then use speed to point upwind. A skiff-style dinghy which planes upwind must be sailed free for maximum VMG.

- The rudder should have slight weather helm to help provide lift to windward. If weather helm feels too heavy, the boat is probably heeling over too far. If the boat is sailing upright, the mainsail leech may be too tight or the centreboard/daggerboard may need to be partly lifted as the wind increases. If the boat has lee helm (bearing away), the rig may require more power with tighter leeches.

- When sailing through waves, move crew weight slightly aft to prevent pitching. On a double-handed boat, both crew must be close together. Increased camber (fuller sails) will help the boat to power through waves, with twist to make the sails more controllable as the boat changes speed on wave faces.

Like all modern dinghies, the RS200 is designed to be sailed upright. The crew must move weight aft if the bows get stopped by waves. The venue is Lake Garda which gets a lot of wind blown chop when the Ora creates wonderful Force 4-5 conditions on most summer afternoons.

Sail control

- The mast should be straight and raked upright for maximum power. Check with the class-tuning guide for recommended rig settings. Sails should be deeper (increased camber) with more tension in the leech to enhance pointing.

- Use the mainsheet and jib sheets to control leech tension which will affect how high the boat can point. The boom should be pulled in to the centreline of the boat, unless there is too much power in the mainsail. If the top windward telltale stops streaming, it indicates the mainsail is becoming overpowered and needs more twist to exhaust air flow over the leech.

- If the boat feels slow and the sails appear to have stalled, ease sheets to increase power and allow the boat to bear away by a few degrees.

- Do not let the boat heel when a gust hits. Keep the boat driving forward by easing the mainsheet and if necessary luff slightly into the gust, but without losing any speed.

- Take slack out of the kicking strap but do not pull on tension, which would bend the mast and depower the mainsail. You want all the power available, with a small amount of twist in the mainsail to promote airflow.

- No tension is required in the Cunningham if you can hold the boat upright. Creases can normally be left in the mainsail without inhibiting performance. Cunningham tension will bend the mast and open the upper leech of the mainsail, reducing power and ability to point upwind.

- Ease the outhaul slightly to increase power in the mainsail, which should have full camber (horizontal curve) for maximum power.

- Watch the telltales on the windward side of the jib which should start lifting, when sailing upwind. As the wind increases, move jib cars slightly forward to provide more tension on the jib leech.

Top Tip

- If you can't point, it may be because you are sailing in another boat's dirty wind. Alternately, your rig set-up may be incorrect. Check it against other boats of the same type and class recommendations. Another possibility is that your sails have stretched out of shape, or there may be drag from your hull or foils being in poor condition.

Poetry in motion! A Merlin Rocket beautifully set up for a Force 4 beam reach. Note how the corners of the spinnaker are absolutely level.

1. Crew hike to hold boat upright when sailing upwind.

2. Keep weight forward unless there are waves.

3. Centreboard or daggerboard fully down.

4. Mast straight for maximum power for as long as the crew can hold the boat down.

5. Pull slack out of kicking strap, but do not tension. Aim to sail with a small amount of twist in the mainsail.

6. No Cunningham tension required unless rig is overpowered.

7. Ease the outhaul for maximum mainsail power.

8. Full sail for maximum power.

9. Leech telltales streaming.

10. Windward jib telltales just lifting.

22 | Strong Wind Performance

Racing in Force 4 and above, when the rig starts to develop excessive power and good boat handling can make huge differences to comparative speed...

Jonny McGovern and Tom Mapplebeck race with the 470 class on a tough day at the Holland Regatta, held on the North Sea in May each year.

Charlotte Dobson rounds a mark in high winds at the World Sailing Championships in Portugal.

Sail control

- Flatten the sails and give them more twist to reduce power. If the mast has adjustable rake, raking it aft will reduce power. Check individual class recommendations which should give advice on setting up the rig for different crew weights.

- You will need to play the mainsheet, easing during gusts and sheeting in during lulls to maintain a direct course without loss of speed to windward. In strong gusts it may be necessary to ease both mainsail and jib, in order to keep the jib slot open with no increase in power.

- If you need to luff and slow down in gusts, the rig has too much power.

- If the mainsail is backwinding, it may be slowing you down. The solution its to reduce power by flattening the sail and increasing twist.

- Balance and boat speed need to be finely matched when sailing upwind. If the boat slows down, heeling forces will increase so the boat heels right over and slows down to a crawl. Ease the mainsheet to maintain speed upwind with the boat held upright; bear off a few degrees if the boat feels

Position

- If you are fully hiked out or on the trapeze and still can't hold the boat upright, it is vital to depower the rig. Do not let the boat heel right over in gusts – it will just slow down or slide sideways. Plus, you may lose control as it turns up into the wind due to heavy weather helm and the rudder lifting out of the water.

- Keep weight forward upwind, but adjust weight aft to prevent the bows diving down and slowing the boat. As soon as the boat is planing, move weight well aft to counteract forward forces in the rig. The faster you are sailing, the further back your weight needs to be in the boat.

quicker and more comfortable. The main aim is to keep driving upwind, rather than pointing high and sailing slowly. Skiff-style dinghies must be sailed free and fast, staying bolt upright in order to plane at lightning speed upwind.

- Use full kicking strap tension to bend the mast and flatten the sail. The kicking strap will also help to control leech twist as you play the mainsheet, by holding the boom down. If the boom lifts when you ease the mainsheet, the sails will develop increased power and make the boat want to heel over more.

- Use full Cunningham tension to compress and bend the mast. This will flatten the sail and move draft forward. It will also twist open the leech in the upper part of the sail, which will act like a flat blade with no power in the top of the sail.

- Tension the outhaul to flatten and depower the mainsail. However, increased camber (fullness) may be required to provide power low down when sailing through waves.

- Tensioning the luff will help flatten the jib. Move jib sheet cars aft to reduce tension on the jib leech and increase tension on the foot. This will twist the top of the leech and depower the jib. If barber-haulers are fitted, move the jib sheet leads outboard to open up the slot and reduce airflow between the mainsail and jib.

- Part-raising the centreboard or daggerboard reduces lateral forces pressing against the foil under the hull. In stronger winds, this can be useful to prevent the boat heeling. Leeway should not be a problem, as the fully powered rig drives the boat forwards at close to maximum upwind speed.

Top Tip

Be cautious at the start in strong winds. Do not risk capsizing with a gybe during the count-down from five minutes! If you try sitting on the line, beware that your boat will quickly get blown sideways and it is impossible to maintain the same position without sheeting in and driving forwards.

Heeling force

Sideways Force

A **B**

WIND

Partly raising the board reduces lateral resistance under the hull and can make it easier to hold the boat upright in strong winds.

Nick Rogers and Joe Glanfield power their 470 downwind in big waves during Hyeres Olympic Sailing Week.

Full power offwind

- Apparent wind means that the faster your boat is travelling, the less pressure there will be in the sails, effectively making the boat easier to control at higher speeds.

- Go for maximum power when sailing offwind. Bear away to handle excess power during gusts and prevent the boat heeling; then head up in the lulls, to 'heat up' the power some more.

- Keep the boat flat. Do not let it heel. Luffing out of control happens much more quickly if the boat heels when sailing at speed.

- If the boat rolls to windward, it may capsize on top of you. To prevent this, sheet in on the main or luff onto a higher course.

- On some dinghies it's normal to retract the centreboard or daggerboard for less drag when sailing downwind. However, rolling on waves can be reduced by having the board part-way down. Use small tiller movement to keep the boat steering in gentle curves and do not move around the cockpit to try to prevent the rolls – they will get worse!

- If you want to lose power when sailing offwind, ease the kicking strap to let the boom rise up and depower the mainsail which will twist.

- Running by the lee should provide the shortest course to the leeward mark. However, gybing from broad reach to broad reach downwind may provide superior VMG in difficult conditions, and will almost certainly be more fun!

Stevie Morrison and Ben Rhodes race their 49er at full bore in the Holland Regatta held on rough water on the North Sea.

1. The boat is held upright with the crew fully hiked.
2. Weight moved back to lift the bow over waves.
3. Board may need to be partly raised to reduce heeling.
4. Mast raked back to reduce power in the mainsail.
5. Full kicking strap tension to bend the mast and flatten the mainsail.
6. Full Cunningham tension to flatten the sail. This will help to twist the top half open and move power forward in the sail.
7. Tight outhaul to depower the mainsail, but a fuller foot shape may be needed for sailing through waves.
8. Flat mainsail for minimum upwind power.
9. Leech telltales streaming.
10. Luff telltales just streaming on the jib with sheet lead adjusted to open slot.

Top Tip

Waves can provide a very fast downwind ride. Don't waste them by sailing in a straight line which follows the waves. Luff or bear away to boost speed and prolong the ride on each wave face, moving body weight to windward or leeward to ensure the boat stays upright and can plane at full bore.

23 | Top Turns

Fast tacks and failsafe gybes are vital during a race. These are techniques that require a lot of practice in every wind strength. Follow the example of Ben Ainslie – with 30 minutes to spare after one training session, he dedicated the time to tacking every 30 seconds!

Fast and fluid tacks

Tacking with a centre mainsheet, the helm always pivots facing forward while moving from side to side. Good technique is required to change hands during the tack, while keeping control of the tiller and mainsheet. This requires a lot of practice. Problems are often caused by not sitting far enough forward to flip the tiller extension into the new sailing position.

1. Hold the tiller extension across the front of your body, using a 'dagger' grip with the backhand.

2. Uncleat the mainsheet to ease the mainsail as you steer into the tack.

3. Stand up and pivot through 180 degrees, facing forwards, as you cross the cockpit. Keep the mainsheet in your front hand and continue to steer the boat through the tack with your back hand.

4. Let your hand swivel around the tiller extension as you move to the new side. You will also need to angle the tiller extension, to ensure it can fit through the gap between cockpit, mainsheet and boom.

5. Move onto the new side, holding the tiller extension with the same hand, which is now crossed behind your back, while your other hand continues to hold the mainsheet.

6. Sheet in and get the boat settled on the new tack, sailing in the right direction and not heeling over.

7. When you're ready for the hand transfer, move the mainsheet hand onto the lower part of the tiller extension. Then immediately flick the tiller extension across the front of your body and grab the sheet with your new front hand.

1-2. Swivel the tiller extension so it passes under the boom.

3-4. Face forward as you move to the new side.

5. Sit out while holding the tiller extension behind your back.

6-7. Transfer hands and pull the boat upright.

1. Steer gently into the tack in light winds.

2. Both crew roll the boat as the boat turns head to wind.

3. Move across with the mainsheet eased as the boat rolls through the turn.

4. Flatten the boat and sheet in to power up on the new tack.

Roll tacks

In lighter winds, it can pay to tack frequently and fast, to make the most of every wind shift. This is particularly true when racing inland, with wind coming from all over the place! Roll tacking produces a quicker and more powerful turn, with aggressive use of crew weight helping to spin the boat through the tack. By rolling the boat with your body weight, the sails are fanned through the air. This keeps them filled for longer with less drag created by the sails flapping, so that air flow is re-attached and powers up the sails more quickly after the tack. In very light winds, the tack is likely to start with the helm sitting to windward and the crew sitting to leeward to balance the boat.

1. Steer gently into the tack, allowing the forces created by heeling to leeward to turn the boat towards the wind.

2. The crew joins the helm on the windward side to roll the boat into the tack, as the boom crosses the centreline with sails head to wind.

3. As the sails collapse, the helm moves across the cockpit and eases the mainsheet, while the crew starts sheeting in on the new side. The forces on the rig help swing the bows away from the wind and onto the new course.

4. The boat will be pointing in the right direction, but heeling right over to leeward on the new tack. The helm sits out on the windward side-deck to flatten the boat – with or without the crew's help – while sheeting in to accelerate the boat back up to the speed with which it entered the tack. Lean out and sheet in the sails in one dynamic movement, bringing the boat upright and powering it up at the same time.

5. The crew may then need to return to leeward position for light wind beating.

Can't tack round in a blow

If you have problems getting the boat to tack in stronger winds, you are probably coming off the side deck and easing the mainsheet too soon, in order to prevent the boat heeling right over. The problem is that sheeting out will reduce weather helm – the boat's natural tendency to turn into the wind – so the tack requires much more use of the rudder. But the rudder provides a brake, which slows the boat right down as the bows swing towards the wind. Next thing, the boat stalls on a wave and starts moving backwards. The best way to avoid this is to keep power on for as long as possible:

1. Wait until the boat has turned head to wind, before you move off the side deck (or trapeze) and into the cockpit. This will ensure you can keep the mainsheet pulled in, with the leech of the sail helping to drive the boat round.

2. Free off some mainsheet when the mainsail starts back winding.

3. Do not sheet in until the boat is on the new course, with the crew starting to hike or go out on the trapeze. This will ensure the boat does not heel too far to leeward when you pull in the mainsheet to power up the boat.

Fast and failsafe gybes

During a tack, the boat turns into the wind and loses most of the power in its sails. During a gybe, the boat turns away from the wind, so sails are powered up throughout the turn. Gybing in light winds is easy, but becomes a much more dynamic manoeuvre in stronger winds – particularly when close to other boats, in the heat of a race. If you make a mistake, it's easy to capsize and lose any chance of winning that race.

The perfect gybe

Skiff sailors always walk when they tack or gybe – good technique avoids it becoming a 'walk on the wild side.'

• Steer carefully through the turn – always be in full control of the rudder. Use continuous adjustment rather than one large rudder movement.

• Keep the boat flat throughout the gybe – you may let the boat heel slightly to windward going into the gybe, to help it bear away. Sheeting in slightly helps power up the sail as the boat turns.

• As soon as you are running by the lee (wind blowing over the new windward side of the stern), you can induce the mainsail to gybe by giving a sharp tug on the falls of the mainsheet. Some dinghies have a 'gybing strop' attached to the boom for this purpose. If it won't gybe, you need to keep the boat turning. With experience it's possible to judge the right moment, as pressure goes light in the mainsail.

• If you leave the boom to decide when it's time to gybe, it may wait until the boat has turned far enough for the wind to backwind the mainsail. That's OK in light winds, but in strong winds the boom will swing across and crash to the new side. The boat heels over, the helm loses control of steering and the boat keeps turning onto a beam reach leading to inevitable capsize.

• As soon as the mainsail flicks across, straighten out the rudder on the new course, while the boat is still sailing deep downwind. Do not let the boat round up onto a reach, which will blow it onto its side.

• The helmsman pivots round to the new windward side of the boat, using the same hand technique as for tacking. Sit well forward with the tiller extension held behind your back, grab the lower half of the tiller extension with your old sheet hand, flick the tiller extension across the front of your body, and grab the mainsheet with your new front hand to complete the gybe.

• If you are sailing double-handed, the crew moves into the cockpit during the gybe, but may need to move weight quickly to flatten the boat if the helm has less than perfect control. Let off the jib sheet and pull in on the new side as the boom swings across the cockpit, if necessary changing from goosewing to goosewing on the windward side.

Gybing

1. Go into the gybe at full speed. Slowing down will load up the rig.

2. Keep the boat flat or heel to windward to help the turn.

3. Flip the tiller extension to steer through the turn.

4. Straighten up to head downwind as the boom swings across.

5. Keep the boat flat and sailing straight during the critical part of the gybe.

6. Power up on the new course and change hands.

Gybing in strong winds

- Keep control by gybing through the smallest possible angle. You only need to turn the boat through an arc that's big enough to gybe the mainsail. From there you can get the boat under control and choose where you want to sail – either keep running downwind or head up onto a reach. A wider gybe angle will require a greater course correction.

- If you lose speed – normally while failing to gybe the mainsail – apparent wind will load up in the rig and makes things difficult to handle. Safest policy is to get back on your original course, settle down, draw breath and then try to gybe again.

> ### Top Tip
> The faster you sail through the gybe, the lighter the apparent wind will be on the rig, which should make it easier to control the sail. If the boat slows down, apparent wind will increase and make it more difficult to control the sail.

Board up or down for the gybe?

- On traditional dinghy classes, gybe from run to run with the centreboard partly or fully retracted. If it's down, the boat may 'trip' due to water pressure on the board, which will make it heel right over.

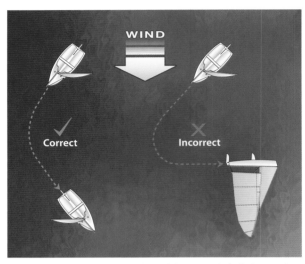

Gybe through the smallest possible angle in strong winds, before coming onto your new course. If you attempt to gybe through a wide angle, the boat will blow over. If in doubt, steer downwind.

- On single-handed dinghies such as the Laser, gybe with the daggerboard partly retracted. Make sure the top of the board is clear of the kicking strap.

- On modern dinghies with asymmetric spinnakers, it's normal to leave the centreboard or daggerboard fully down.

1. OK world champion Nick Craig rolls to windward for a tight gybe.

Roll gybes

In lighter winds, try a downwind variation on the roll tack, using pronounced windward heel to initiate the turn. The roll gybe must provide a continuous smooth transition.

- Roll the boat to windward to assist bearing away.

- Grab the falls of the mainsheet and pull the boom across with a positive tug when the leech of the mainsail starts back winding.

- Centralise the tiller and balance the boat, while lining up for the new course.

2. Nick ducks under the low boom and straightens the rudder…

3. … then flattens the boat on the new course, ready to change hands.

Phew! Even a gold medallist can look a little unsure in strong winds. Paul Goodison, the Olympic Gold Medallist, ducks under the boom at the mid point of a gybe. The tiller is almost dead centre, with the turn dictated by the angle at which the Laser is heeling.

24 | Hike Hard

You've got to keep the boat upright to sail consistently fast round the course, with perfect balance and control. Effective use of hiking is vital when racing to the windward mark – the more effective the leverage, the sooner you will arrive…

Hiking style

- How you hike will depend on the dinghy you race. Some designs have beautifully contoured side decks, which can almost make hiking a pleasure. Others have wide, flat side decks with hard angles, which make hiking a tough proposition.

- Cockpit ergonomics need to match your physique. If you are way too short or way too tall for the boat, hiking will feel very uncomfortable.

- Many dinghies have adjustable toe straps for different leg length crews, or for the difference in sailing on flat water or waves. If the toe strap is too long, your legs will be too bent. If the toe strap is too short, you will not be able to get enough weight out of the boat. Adjust toe strap length until it feels just right for the conditions, with the gunwale approximately halfway down your thigh. You need to find a position that can be maintained for the duration of the race, with legs and back as straight as possible for maximum leverage.

"Grrrr!" Steve Cockerell shows the attitude that made him Streaker National Champion.

True grit

- The harder you hike, the faster you can drive the boat. It's no good depowering the rig, so you can sit comfortably on the side deck with the boat held upright – crews who are hiking harder can sail faster.

- Be ready to make a major hiking effort at the start of the race, when it is vital to get clear of dirty wind by outpacing boats to windward and leeward. After that, it may not be possible to hike hard all the way up the beat, but at least you have all the advantages of a clean start.

- Hiking relies on strong leg muscles, strong stomach muscles and good position. If it feels tough, console yourself with the thought that it's a wonderful way to tone your body. After a hard season's hiking, you'll look great on the beach!

- Padded toe straps and good dinghy boots with reinforced tops will make hiking more comfortable. Wearing neoprene hiking shorts, with battens and pads to spread the load as you lean out from the side deck, might almost make hiking a pleasure.

Time to bear away and flatten the boat – you can't just do it by hiking.

Paul Goodison sails perfectly flat with his bottom just lifted off the waves. Not so easy as it looks!

Using the lever

• Hiking applies a simple lever to keep the boat upright. The longer the lever, the more effective your hiking will be. When possible, go for a full stretch hike – feet under a short toe strap, legs slightly bent, with upper body held straight and almost parallel with the water.

• Do not drop your backside over the side of the boat and sit upright. This position is uncomfortable and relatively ineffective, with a much reduced lever due to your upper body being too close to the boat.

• Hiking flat out poses problems in waves. If your body keeps hitting the water, it will slow the boat down. Try hiking with a longer toe strap and more bend in your knees, for a less extended and slightly more upright hiking position. This will provide greater upper body mobility, allowing you to move your shoulders forwards to push down the bows, or back to lift the bows over the wave. For this kind of upper body movement, your feet need to be firmly locked under the toe strap and stable.

Out for a blast in a British Moth – the helm bears away to flatten the boat.

25 | On the Wire

Racing on a trapeze boat is brilliant. You not only get a superb feeling of power, but also enjoy a wonderful view of the race. The disadvantage is that you're more locked in than hiking – tacking on wind shifts requires greater effort and takes more time.

Frances Peters and Gemma McIntyre enjoy sailing trials with a big rig version of the RS800, developed as a potential Olympic twin wire dinghy class for girls.

Trapezing height

On many dinghies, the trapeze rings can be adjusted for height while sailing, by pulling a control line through a cleat to vary the length between the trapeze ring and wire. The lower you trapeze, the more effective your leverage will be – flat out and virtually parallel to the water provides the maximum lever. However, you may need to pull the trapeze ring higher so that your body clears waves, or lower to maintain a comfortable position when standing at the back of the boat on a downwind reach. When you first learn trapezing, it's much easier with a high hook position.

Go as low as you can. Trapezing horizontally provides the most effective leverage, but is difficult. The helm may need a higher position to see over the crew. Both crew may need a higher position for waves.

Going out on the wire

The trapeze wire will always tend to pull your forwards, so lead with your front foot and use it to brace on the side of the boat. The front leg will support most of your weight, while the back leg provides balance if you need to lean back.

- Grab the plastic handle above the trapeze ring with your front hand and hook on with your back hand.

- Take your weight on the trapeze wire and move out onto the side of the boat or its rack, taking the jib sheet or spinnaker sheet with you. If the wire is still too slack, adjust the ring to a higher position.

- Step out of the boat with your front foot, without over-sheeting the jib or spinnaker.

- Follow with your back foot and relax into the harness, before letting go of the handle.

- Keep your legs straight with your feet close together.

The helm sits in, allowing the crew to stay out on the wire and trim the kite.

Bending or straightening your legs keeps the boat sailing level in a gusty breeze.

Staying out on the wire

Relax with your weight on the wire. It's a lot more comfortable and efficient than hiking, and provides a great viewpoint to look around the course.

- Stand with the balls of your feet on the side of the boat or rack. Look ahead and keep your feet close together. Use your front leg as a brace, with your back leg slightly bent and relaxed.

- Holding the jib or spinnaker sheet will help maintain your balance. If you lose balance and start swinging forwards, it's OK to grab the helmsman's shoulder – his buoyancy aid will provide a useful emergency hand-hold, but not his hair!

- Normal position is to stand just behind the shroud when beating upwind. Step back when the boat bears away onto a reach, keeping your front legs braced against increased forward pull from both the trapeze wire and the jib or spinnaker sheet.

- If you keep thumping into waves, you may get washed off the side of the boat. Pull the trapeze ring to a higher position.

- If there are lulls and gusts, the helm may move in and out of the cockpit to keep the crew out on the wire. The crew can move in and out by bending and straightening his legs, making sure the boat does not roll over to windward.

"Woa!" Time to cool things down. It gets tricky to maintain balance on the wire if you let the boat heel too far.

Coming in off the wire

Just reverse going out on the wire to get back onto the boat.

- Bend your front leg, while holding the jib or spinnaker sheet in your back hand, which will provide support as you swing into the boat.

- Move the back foot off the side of the boat or rack and into the cockpit, supporting your body with your back hand.

- Follow immediately with your front foot, so you are crouching in a semi-hiking position.

- Knock the trapeze ring off the hook with your back hand; let go of the handle with your front hand.

Trapezing in marginal winds can be uncomfortable – be prepared to slide in over the side deck.

Wire-to-wire

Tacking or gybing from 'wire-to-wire' is fast and efficient. When tacking, the object is to stay out for as long as possible on the old tack, so the boat rolls to windward and powers up the turn.

- Just before the helm steers into the tack, the crew grabs the trapeze handle to hold his body weight and slips off the hook, while still hanging fully extended on the wire. (If you stay hooked in, there is a good chance of getting stuck while the boat rolls over on top of you.)

- Come in off the wire and step across the cockpit as the helm steers past head-to-wind.

- Take the new jib sheet in your back hand and grab the trapeze handle with your front hand as you pivot (facing forward) onto the new side.

- Step out and go horizontal on the wire, supporting your full weight with your front arm.

- Hook on and let go of the handle.

Katrina Hughes prepares to go wire-to-wire in a tack. All her weight is taken on the front hand.

Skiff trapezing

When sailing an asymmetric skiff, it's most efficient for both crew to walk across the cockpit during tacks and gybes. This requires hooking in or out of the trapeze while standing on the side of the boat or racks, without any time wasted by crouching or sliding into the cockpit. If you're sailing a skiff, you never sit down!

1. Dave Hall and Mari Shepherd go for a twin wire tack on the 29erXX.

2. Dave walks across as Mari clips on…

3. … ready to go out as Dave sheets in.

4. With power on, Dave joins Mari on the wire.

Single-handed on the wire provides a great sensation – the RS700 also flies a kite downwind.

Helming on the wire

Dinghies such as the RS800 race with both crews on the wire for double the fun, with none of the hardship of hiking. A few extra ground rules will be required to get round the race track on a twin wire boat.

- It's less easy for the helm to go in and out on the wire, primarily because he is steering. If wind pressure is variable, the crew should be prepared to go in and out while the helm stays stable.

- After a tack, the crew will normally go out on the wire ahead of the helm who is occupied by steering the boat. One problem is maintaining a straight course. When you hook in and go out, the natural tendency is to take the tiller extension with you, which will make the boat bear away and power up the sails. Be ready to slide your hand along the extension or lock it against the rack.

- Twin-wire dinghies will tend to get maximum VMG downwind, with both crew on the wire during a spinnaker reach. But in strong winds and waves, the helm may find it easier to control the boat by sitting in and sailing deeper to hold the boat flat. After all, you will get to the leeward mark a lot quicker if you don't capsize. The same is true for a trapeze single-hander with a spinnaker, such as the RS700 or Musto Skiff. Stay out for maximum VMG if you can handle it; come in and sail deeper if boat control becomes an issue.

- Who gets the best view? The helm should trapeze higher than the crew. This will provide an unobstructed view ahead, also helping to ensure that the helm does not get knocked off by a wave – a catastrophic recipe for a capsize!

RS800 Eurocup action on Lake Garda. Helming on the wire, you need a clear view forward. It's best to look over the top of the crew.

Sail safe

Virtually all fatal accidents during dinghy races have been due to a sailor getting trapped under a capsized boat which has inverted. One specific problem which has been identified is the trapeze hook catching on part of the boat – for instance hooking onto a shroud. ISAF has introduced a Racing Rule 40.2 which states that 'A trapeze or hiking harness shall have a device capable of quickly releasing the competitor from the boat at all times while in use'. The most effective solution is a quick-release hook that detaches from the spreader bar by pressing a button or pulling a toggle.

Modern boats are prone to inversion due to their wide beam and high buoyancy. Getting trapped by your trapeze hook is a freak accident that can be alleviated by a quick release hook system. In this shot, the helm is pulling in the spinnaker while the crew holds the daggerboard of an RS800.

26 | Capsize Recovery

Sod's law ensures you will capsize at the worst possible moment during a race – just before the start, at the windward mark, or gybing at the bottom of the course. You've got to flip the boat back up and continue racing with minimum delay…

Floating high

Most modern dinghies have a self-draining cockpit, which is both a boon and a bane. The boon is that any water in the cockpit floods straight out over the transom; the bane is that the volume and depth of a self-draining cockpit will make the hull float high if it capsizes, which can easily lead to full inversion.

Keep it dry

As the boat falls on its side, the helm (or crew) should do their utmost to make it a dry capsize. Flick one leg over to straddle the side of the boat. Then flick over the other leg and slide onto the centreboard or daggerboard. You can then grab the gunwale with both hands and flip the boat back upright, with little time wasted in the race.

158

With no time to hop over the side on a wild downwind capsize, Charlotte Dobson's Laser Radial inverts on a Force 6 day.

When you reach the point of no return, it's time to hop over the side and step smartly on the centreboard. You may not even get wet!

Scoop your crew

• If you are racing double-handed, the crew will normally (but not always) be down in the water. There is not room for two on the board!

• The crew's role is to make sure sheets are running free before you start trying to right the boat. Letting off the kicking strap will also help depower the mainsail. If the spinnaker was hoisted when you capsized, it must be pulled back into its chute or bundled into its bag.

• Use the scoop method to get the crew back into the cockpit as the boat is pulled upright. While the helm leans back on the board to lift the rig and start righting the boat, the crew floats alongside the front half of the cockpit, waiting to roll inside as the boat comes upright. It is vital that the crew does not to grab hold of something in the cockpit too early, which may pull the boat back down when it is half righted. If all goes well, the crew will be inside the cockpit on the leeward side, while the helm steps over the windward side, with both of them balancing the boat.

The crew drops in the water while the helm hops over the side. One has to be unlucky! If you're down in the water, don't pull down on the boat. or push down on the rig, which will risk inverting the boat and make it much slower to recover from the capsize.

The helm stands on the board to hold the boat level and prevent inversion. The crew makes sure all sheets are running free. If the spinnaker is out, it must be pulled inside the chute.

The helm pulls back to right the boat, scooping up the crew on the leeward side where she can roll into the cockpit. Unlike the crew, the lucky helm stays dry throughout the whole procedure!

Don't let it go right **over**

If the boat looks ready to invert, the crew should keep clear by holding on to the stern. Never stand on the rig or pull down on the topside, which will help turn the boat upside-down.

- Hang onto a line to make sure you don't lose the boat. Trying to grab hold of a smooth, slippery dinghy hull is hopeless and it may start to blow downwind faster than you can swim.

- While one crew holds on at the stern, the other can swim round the bottom of the hull to climb onto the centreboard or daggerboard. In some situations the board may be too floating high, or you may be too exhausted get up there. If your dinghy has righting lines under the gunwales, this is a good time to use them.

Get weight off the top before you pull it over and invert the boat. Just let go and fall in the water.

If the boat inverts

- A classic single-bottomed dinghy will normally have an air pocket inside the cockpit when it is inverted. A modern double-bottomed dinghy may have no effective air pocket, which is a potential danger.

- If you capsize while racing a double-handed boat, both crew should first ensure their partner is OK.

- If you are stuck under the mainsail, move back towards the leech, which is the easiest way out and also gives you something to grab hold of. While a Dacron© mainsail is fairly easy to push up off the surface, a laminate Mylar© sail forms a more rigid barrier – particularly with full length battens.

- If one crew is seriously stuck under the boat or sail and you cannot pull the boat upright, there are two courses of action:

1. Signal to a safety boat for immediate assistance.

2. Get down in the water and help. It's possible a loose elastic or control line traps the crew. Be prepared to use your safety knife to cut it free. If the trapeze hook is caught, activate the quick release buckle and do your best to help them to get free.

"What do we do next?" An upturned boat is surprisingly buoyant and stable to stand on. Make sure the daggerboard does not fall down through the slot – you will need it fully extended to pull the boat back upright, while standing on the underside of the gunwale.

Righting from an inversion

- Both crew can climb up on the underside of the windward gunwale, then lean back on the board to start pulling the rig to a horizontal position. It may be necessary to use a rope, such as the jib sheet, as a temporary righting line.
- When the top of the board is within reach, the heavier crew should climb onto it and continue pulling back until the mast is on the surface and pointing downwind.
- With the rig held in a stable horizontal position, the other crew can swim round to the cockpit and prepare to be scooped.

Wind direction

- In most conditions it's easiest to right a boat with the bows pointing towards the wind. It may help to swim the bows in the right direction.
- When the hull is floating high on its side, it will tend to blow downwind of the rig, which acts as a sea anchor. If you right the boat from this position, the boat may roll through a complete 180 degrees and capsize the other way. To avoid this problem, get the crew to hang onto a toe strap which will prevent the boat coming fully upright. Lean back on the board until the head of the mainsail is just clear of the surface. Hold the boat in this position, and allow the wind to swivel the rig in a downwind arc. Choose your moment when the wind is blowing towards your side of the bows to pull the boat fully upright.

What happens if you capsize on the trapeze?

- Crouch down as the boat goes over, unhook from the trapeze and slide down the hull. If possible get straight onto the centreboard or daggerboard.
- Do not fall forwards onto the sail – you may fall straight through it. Get weight off the topside and off the rig as soon as possible to avoid turning the boat upside-down.
- If the boat capsizes to windward, get the hook off the trapeze ring as the rig falls on top of you. To get out from under the sail, move back towards the leech which you can push up.

If the boat is going over, keep cool and unhook from the trapeze. Do not fall into the mainsail – you may fall right through it!

Getting back in the race

- On modern dinghies with an open transom, it's normally easiest and most stable to climb back in over the stern.
- Grab the tiller, check the control lines and prepare to rejoin the race. Work out where you were when the capsize happened, where you are now, and where you need to go next. Do not abandon the race unless you are too exhausted to keep sailing. Other people may capsize and lose even more places!

"Allez oop!" When a Laser comes back upright, be prepared to use your weight to best effect to level the boat. Charlotte Dobson shows how to prevent a repeat roll-over during a very windy race.

Success in dinghy racing not only requires good boat speed and boat handling technique. It is a tactical sport in which shifting winds and moving tides play a major role…

Working wind shifts

- Wind is not stable. It keeps changing in direction and strength, particularly when sailing on inland waters where the wind may be funneling around buildings or trees and creating massive turbulence. This means that big advantages can be achieved by being on the tack that gets you closest to the windward mark.

- Changes in wind direction tend to occur during gusts and lulls, and keen eyed sailors will spot the effect on the water before the new wind direction hits their sails. You should be ready to tack if the wind heads you. This means the wind direction swings more directly onto the bows (to leeward), forcing the boat to bear away, which will take it further from the windward mark. But if the wind lifts, the wind direction will swing away from the bows (to windward), allowing the boat to head up and sail a more direct course to the windward mark.

- When a boat tacks on a header, the wind may soon oscillate back. Be prepared to tack quickly if the wind heads you again, with the object of steadily getting closer to the windward mark.

- When sailing downwind, reverse the procedure by staying with headers and gybing on lifters to get closer to the leeward mark.

1. A and B are sailing almost level.
2. A attacks on a header so it is sailing more directly towards the windward mark. B does not tack and is sailing less directly towards the windward mark.
3. The wind shifts back to its original direction. A tacks back onto starboard, with a clear gain over B.

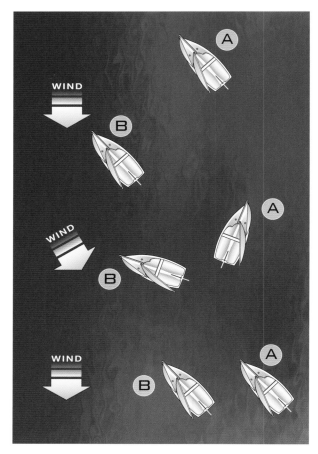

Which tack is pointing closest to the windward mark? Wind shifts can determine who gets there first, particularly when racing on a confined stretch of water – this is Frensham Pond in Surrey

The Finn, RS200 and Laser are all pointing at different angles. With no boats ahead, the Laser has clearly been headed, but will need to wait for the other two to tack as port tack becomes favourable.

Oscillating or persistent?

- It is important to identify whether a shift is oscillating or persistent. Each requires a different strategy.

- An oscillating wind moves in a series of shifts about a mean direction. A persistent shift – typically a sea breeze that will start blowing towards the shore – moves in one general direction, but may oscillate.

- A persistent shift will favour one side of the course as the wind direction changes. An oscillating shift will favour sailors who tack on every header, in order to sail a shorter course to the windward mark.

- If you are lifted in an oscillating shift, stay on that tack as you are being lifted. If you are lifted in a persistent shift, best strategy will be to tack in order to get to the inside of the wind bend being created by the persistent shift.

Which side is favoured?

- Boats can tack out to both sides of the course, and the wind will not blow at the same strength across the whole area. Sailing up the side with the most wind or the most favourable tide can make significant gains.

- In light winds try to sail in strongest pressure and don't be too concerned about wind direction. You may get much better VMG sailing at 5 knots 15 degrees off course, than sailing at 1 knot in the correct direction. In medium or strong winds, choosing the best wind direction becomes more important than chasing wind pressure.

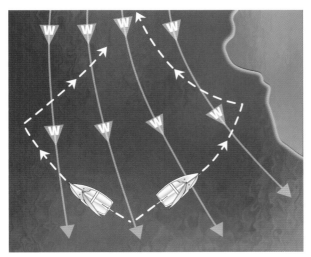

A persistent shift such as a sea breeze moves in one general direction, which will favour one side of the course. Sailing to the inside of the bend (towards land in this illustration) is the top tactical choice.

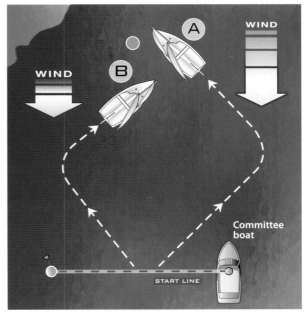

One side of the beat may be favoured by wind and tide. In this illustration, more wind on the right side helps A to arrive first.

If there are no other critical factors, always sail in the strongest wind pressure for best speed around the course.

Maximise every gust

- Racing downwind, gusts not only provide the opportunity to sail faster but also to sail a lower course, heading more directly to the leeward mark.
- Sailing upwind, gusts may provide the opportunity to sail faster, but are most useful for gaining an advantage as the wind direction shifts.

Heating up

- A summer sea breeze can provide the most perfect conditions for dinghy racing. The combination of light gradient winds created by a high or low-pressure system and a marked temperature difference between sea and land will create a sea breeze. The land heats up quickly during the morning, causing air to rise. Replacement air is drawn towards the coast, producing a sea breeze which normally kicks in during the afternoon and may blow up to Force 4-5, before dying away in early evening.
- If the sea breeze blows in the same direction as the gradient wind, the wind will be strong. If the sea breeze blows against the gradient wind, there may be no wind in the afternoon at all! The sea breeze will tend to veer with the sun throughout the afternoon, and may end up blowing parallel to the coastline by sunset.

Converging and diverging wind

Wind blowing over land is slowed and deflected in the opposite direction to the sun (the wind backs). If wind is on your back and land is on your left, the breeze should diminish as it diverges inland. If the wind is on your back and the land on your right, the breeze should increase as it converges offshore.

All the joys of a summer sea breeze during the RS Feva National Championships in the Solent off Hayling Island.

Be aware of tidal flow. Both boats are heading high for the yellow mark, to avoid being swept downwind by the tide.

Tidal flow

Dinghies sail relatively slowly, so tide can play a major role in speed around the course.

- Before you start racing, check local tide tables which should be posted by the sailing club or are available on the web. Remember to correct for British Summer Time (BST) by adding one hour if required. You need to know the time of low or high water, whether it is spring or neap tides with greater or lesser flow, and how tidal flow is likely to affect the course. For an accurate picture of tidal flow, refer to the tidal diamond on a chart and the associated tide table.

- To assess tide on the course, watch how it flows past a fixed object such as a mooring buoy. Water being pushed up against one side of a buoy will indicate the direction of tidal flow. A small standing wave indicates slow tidal flow; a large standing wave indicates fast tidal flow.

- Look out for headlands, shorelines and the opportunity to escape or use tidal flow to your advantage. For instance, tide flowing round a headland will tend to create a back eddy with reverse flow on the far side.

- Tidal currents run slower in shallow water, which is generally close to the shore. If you have to sail into the tide on one tack, be sure to do so where tidal flow is weakest.

- Beware of tidal flow at the start and on the final approach to marks. If the tide is with you, do not get swept over the line before the start, or over stand the windward mark. If the tide is against you, do not arrive 30 seconds late at the line, or tack too early to lay the windward mark. (The same is true of gybing too early or late for the leeward mark, especially when powered up by a spinnaker.) Caution will normally get you round the course a lot more quickly!

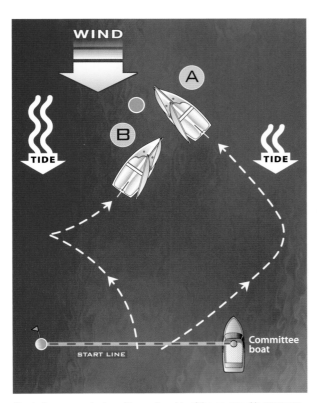

B gets it wrong again, by sailing on the side of the course with strongest contrary tide.

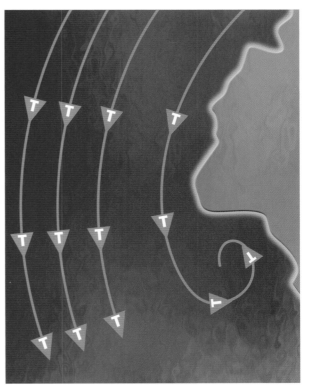

Tidal flow tends to wrap around headlands. This may produce an eddy, with tide flowing in the opposite direction.

With or against?

The combination of wind and tide can have a major impact on conditions round the course. Wind blowing in the same direction as tidal flow will smooth out the surface and should provide an easy ride. Wind blowing against tidal flow (wind against tide) can produce short steep waves, which will slow you down upwind and provide an additional challenge to your ability downwind.

28 Racing with Asymmetric Spinnakers

All the newest racing dinghies have asymmetric spinnakers, which can provide thrilling reach-to-reach racing between the windward and leeward marks, with top performance provided by the apparent wind.

Dave Evans and Rick Peacock enjoy a beautiful blast with the 49ers' 38 square metre kite during the World Sailing Championships in Portugal.

SEIKO
skandia:
TEAM
GBR
RYA
SAIL FOR
GOLD
2008
accenture
GUL
G4S
Group 4 Securicor
SEIKO VELATURA
49er class
VOLVO

28 | Racing with Asymmetric Spinnakers

What an asymmetric does best

- The asymmetric spinnaker (also knows as a gennaker) was originally developed by the Australian 18 foot skiff class and has become standard for all new dinghy designs. Unlike the classic symmetrical spinnaker, the asymmetric has one clew attached to a continuous sheet, which allows the crew to trim on either gybe. The tack is attached to a pole, which is normally pulled out from the bows when the spinnaker is hoisted and retracted when the spinnaker is dropped.

- The asymmetric spinnaker is designed to provide maximum VMG – velocity made good toward the leeward mark on the apparent wind – by gybing from reach to reach on a downwind course.

- Sailing technique is straightforward. Head up towards the wind to heat up the latent power in the spinnaker, then bear away just as the boat starts to heel in order to sail as deep as possible downwind. The harder the wind blows, the deeper you can sail. The helm controls the balance of the boat, by bearing away to prevent the boat heeling to leeward (overpowered) and heading up to prevent the boat heeling to windward (underpowered).

- The asymmetric spinnaker is not designed for running straight downwind, although some asymmetric dinghies such as the RS400 are fitted with a spinnaker pole that can be angled to the windward side to provide more conventional downwind ability. This can be useful when racing on a small inland course, or in lighter winds.

- Attempting to carry an asymmetric spinnaker on a tight reach is a high-risk venture. If a gust hits you will have to bear away and may not be able to sail high enough for the mark. This problem will be compounded if you have to bear away deeper to drop the spinnaker.

- The asymmetric spinnaker needs space to show its pace. A big windward-leeward course on open water is perfect, allowing plenty of room to sail a series of downwind reaches across the rhumb line.

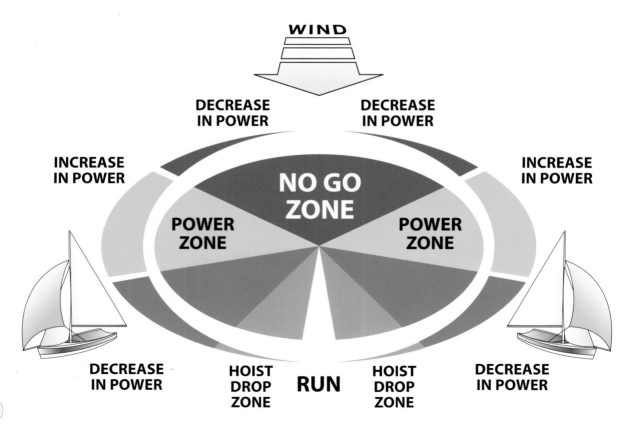

Don't let rip stop rip…

- Spinnakers are made from rip-stop nylon. To ensure there are no rips, any pins, rings or shackles, which the spinnaker may pull against, should be wrapped with a protective layer of insulating tape.

- If the spinnaker jams when you pull it back into the chute, be careful about just pulling harder – you may rip the sail. The most likely cause is that the halyard has jammed in its cleat or is locked by your foot. The alternative solution is to partly rehoist the spinnaker, then pull it back down again.

- Use spinnaker tape to repair small tears and prevent them becoming major rips. Wash salt off the sail and ensure it is completely dry before applying the tape.

Top Tip

- If you have re-rigged the spinnaker, make sure everything is correct with a dry land hoist before you go afloat. Double check with a hoist-gybe-drop sequence on the water before the start.

Watch those spinnakers – they can be fragile!

Going for the hoist

- On the final approach to the windward mark, pull through any slack in the leeward side spinnaker sheet. The helm needs to concentrate on holding the boat flat as it bears away round the windward mark, easing off the mainsheet and moving weight back to prevent the bows diving down. This will allow the crew to move into the cockpit for the hoist. (If the crew has been trimming the mainsheet upwind, he should pass it to the helm as he comes into the boat.)

- Unless the wind is light, the helmsman must bear away deep downwind to ensure the spinnaker is blanketed by the mainsail. Do not risk hoisting on a beam reach across the top of the course, which may allow the partly hoisted spinnaker to fill and blow the boat over sideways. For a safe hoist, wait until you can turn all the way downwind at the spacer mark.

- When hoisting the spinnaker, the crew needs a wide leg stance to pull out maximum lengths of halyard arm over arm, with the aim of getting the spinnaker up and powered as quickly as possible.

- As soon as the spinnaker is hoisted, grab the sheet and go out on the side of the boat – either hiking or on the trapeze – while the helm steers into the wind to power up the sail. If the spinnaker is twisted, try a gybe to pull it straight.

- Make very sure that the spinnaker is fully hoisted. If the head of the sail is not pulled all the way up, the spinnaker will be less effective and could be a lot more difficult to control. One way to be sure is to mark the halyard where it passes through the cleat in the fully up position. You can organise this by doing a dry land hoist.

Standing room only! Simon Hiscocks goes for the hoist while Chris Draper holds their 49er on a level course.

Heating up for optimum VMG

Sailing at full power downwind requires finding the optimum course. Not too low to go slow; not too high to sail too far. Unless the wind is too light to make any use of apparent wind, your course should look like a smoothly snaking wiggle between each gybe. Head up to heat up the power in the spinnaker, then bear away and accelerate on the apparent wind to produce optimum VMG. The boat will only respond to steering with an asymmetric if it is flat. When the boat heels to leeward, bear away immediately to hold it upright while chasing the apparent wind. When the boat heels to windward or starts to slow down, head up to bring back the power.

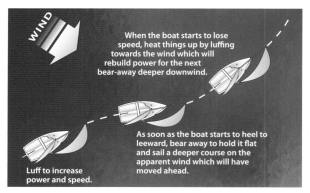

WIND

When the boat starts to lose speed, heat things up by luffing towards the wind which will rebuild power for the next bear-away deeper downwind.

As soon as the boat starts to heel to leeward, bear away to hold it flat and sail a deeper course on the apparent wind which will have moved ahead.

Luff to increase power and speed.

You never sail straight with an asymmetric. Follow a series of bends to match the breeze.

Who does what?

- First, the helm has to steer the boat to hold it flat on the water while driving the boat downwind at maximum speed. This means the helm must steer to follow the spinnaker, as it powers the dinghy offwind. Second, he has to watch for gusts and assess if it's time to gybe on a lifting breeze, which would take you further from the leeward mark. Third, he has to look for traffic, sailing at high speed, with much of the view to leeward obscured by the spinnaker. Remember who has right of way. Port gives way to starboard. A boat sailing downwind must give way to a boat sailing upwind (to windward) on the same tack.

- The crew must concentrate on trimming the spinnaker, which is the boat's downwind powerhouse. The only way to do this is to take the sheet in both hands and look straight at the top half of the luff. Ease the sheet until the luff is just curling. If the sail is over sheeted, indicated by no curl, it will be starved of power. If the luff starts to fold inwards, tweak the sheet in. Aim to keep the luff with a slight curl to ensure maximum power delivery.

Gybing an asymmetric

- It is much easier to gybe an asymmetric than a conventional symmetrical spinnaker. This makes it comparatively effortless to keep gybing with little loss of overall speed – either to pick up a wind shift which lets you sail more directly to the leeward mark, or to escape from another boat's dirty wind.

- The sheet is the only control line that needs to be operated during the gybe. This simplicity allows a rapid transition from fully powered on one gybe to fully powered on the other gybe. The boat keeps moving fast throughout the turn, reducing the danger of the rig loading up with apparent wind.

Gemma McIntyre comes in off the wire on the 29erXX, while Dave Hall stays out to control the boat.

What the helm has to do

- The helmsman should keep the boat as flat as possible throughout the gybe, while concentrating on steering with the boat moving fast to minimise apparent wind. If you slow down to 10 knots when gybing in 20 knots true wind, apparent wind will build to 10 knots. If you let the boat slow to 5 knots, apparent wind will build to 15 knots and make control more difficult as the main boom swings to the new side.

- The boat must be kept upright throughout the gybe. If it's windy, the helm will need to keep steering deep downwind when the boom changes sides, before luffing to build power in the spinnaker with both crew out on the side.

The spinnaker sheet stays fully powered as the crew moves across for the gybe on a 49er.

What the crew has to do

- The asymmetric must be kept under control throughout the gybe. Do not let both sheets go slack, which will allow the spinnaker to fly away from the boat. Always keep the clew pulled back.

- To maintain power and speed, the crew should keep the spinnaker sheet pulled in as he comes in off the side or the trapeze, in order to cross the cockpit.

- Start pulling the new sheet in hand-over-hand, from the middle of the cockpit, while moving out to the new windward side.

- The asymmetric can be slightly over sheeted when the crew starts hiking or goes out on the trapeze. This will allow a small amount of sheet to run out and get the luff curling, as the helm steers to windward to heat up the power, then bears away to continue blasting downhill on the apparent wind.

Going for the drop

Simplicity means you can leave the drop until very close to the leeward mark. The pole retracts automatically as the sail comes down, which means the drop should take little more than 15 seconds. If you drop too early, the boat will slow right down and get overtaken by rivals with spinnakers still hoisted. But if you leave it too late or get a jam in the chute, you'll be sailing upwind with a half-dropped spinnaker pulling the boat sideways. The moral is that a perfectly predictable drop requires practice!

Timing is critical. Drop too late and you will get in a nasty mess. Drop too soon and you will get overtaken. The moral is 'practice makes perfect'.

Top Tip

- Use a lark's head knot to attach the doubled up end of the spinnaker sheet to the clew, and then tie the two free ends of the spinnaker sheet together. This will make a continuous sheet which can be grabbed from anywhere in the cockpit.

What the helm has to do

- Bear away downwind to take pressure out of the spinnaker and allow the crew to move into the middle of the cockpit to pull down the sail, with the mainsail blanketed by the spinnaker.

- Steer wide on the final approach to the mark, then luff through 90 degrees to come out as tight as possible and ensure that the upwind leg starts from the optimum windward position.

What the crew has to do

- As you come in off the side or trapeze, tread on the asymmetric sheet which will keep the spinnaker filling for an extra few seconds while you pull in all the slack on the downhaul line. Alternatively, hand the sheet to the helm. At this point, there should not be much power in the sail.

- Taking slack out of the downhaul pulls the spinnaker back and helps ensure it will get pulled neatly into the chute.

- Uncleat the asymmetric halyard and pull the downhaul line in hand-over-hand as quickly as possible. If something jams, make sure the cleat has not clicked shut, you're not standing on the halyard or that it's not jammed by a tangle of spaghetti.

- Get out on the windward side as the helm turns round the leeward mark. Pull in the jib sheet as you start hiking or go out on the trapeze.

Tie loose ends to the spinnaker sheet together so they can't come undone.

A good way to secure spinnaker sheets to the clew.

Top Tip

Two things can go wrong. Either the spinnaker jams in the chute, or it drops in the water and provides an unwelcome sea anchor, which will surely mess up your race. It is easy to avoid this:

1. Head deep downwind to blanket the spinnaker.

2. Make sure all slack has been taken out of the retrieval line before the drop.

3. Pull in the retrieval line as fast as possible, throwing both hands behind your body as the line comes in.

4. Make sure the halyard, which is a continuous part of the retrieval line, will run free and cannot jam.

If there is still a problem, pull the spinnaker back up and then drop it again.

29 | Racing with Symmetric Spinnakers

The classic style of symmetrical spinnaker is the perfect sail for racing dead downwind, but can also turbo-boost performance on a reaching course. It's a challenging sail to master, which rewards the crew with a major race-winning role.

Nic Asher and Elliot Willis race downhill during the Skandia Sail for Gold Regatta at Weymouth, venue for the 2012 Olympics.

What a symmetric does best

- The symmetrical spinnaker is most effective on a dead run with the spinnaker boom pulled back against the shroud, but can also be flown on a close reach with the spinnaker boom pointing towards the bows.

- The symmetrical spinnaker is considerably more complex than the modern asymmetric. The leeward corner is attached to the sheet which trims the sail. The windward corner is attached to the 'guy' which adjusts the angle of the sail – it should normally be set at approximately 90 degrees to the wind, with both corners level.

- Sheet and guy have the same diameter ropes and are interchangeable between gybes. The spinnaker pole is only attached to the mast when the sail is hoisted, with the guy led through the outer end. The spinnaker pole can be angled backwards or forwards through 90 degrees, or adjusted vertically with the uphaul/downhaul control to ensure both corners of the sail are level.

- The symmetrical spinnaker can be a potent performer inland, particularly when lack of space makes a windward-leeward course impractical. Compared to an asymmetric, it is particularly competitive running directly downwind in lighter breezes.

Sailing on a reach, the pole is lifted to fly both corners level for maximum control.

Mastering the pole

Most dinghies have the pole stowed in hoops alongside the main boom, with the uphaul/downhaul permanently attached so the pole can slide through a ring. From this position, the crew can clip in the guy and push the pole forward on the windward side, then clip the inner end to the mast. When the spinnaker is dropped, the pole is pulled back alongside the boom.

The outer end of the pole slides along the guy (windward sheet) until it meets the clew. The middle is supported by the uphaul/downhaul line. The inner end is attached to the mast.

Look behind you! Nick Rogers and Joe Glanfield need to find clean air to power up that kite.

Going for the hoist

Some dinghies have a chute in front of the jib, which allows the hoist to be made on either tack. Other dinghies have a spinnaker bag in the front of the cockpit, which means that it is advisable to hoist from the leeward side, where the mainsail will blanket the spinnaker. Most dinghies have alternative bags on either side of the mast. This allows the crew to think ahead and drop the spinnaker on the favoured side for the next hoist.

- Sail deep downwind, so the crew can move into the cockpit and the mainsail will blanket and depower the spinnaker on the leeward side during the hoist.

- Pull the spinnaker pole forward and clip the outer end to the guy. Then clip the inner end to the mast, with the uphaul/downhaul sliding to the middle of the pole.

- A symmetric is normally smaller than an asymmetric, so the hoist will be quicker. However there are three lines for the crew to control – halyard, sheet and guy. One popular method is for the helmsman to pull up the halyard hand-over-hand, standing in the cockpit with the tiller pinned between his legs. This leaves the crew free to pull back on the guy and pull in the sheet as the spinnaker is hoisted.

- If the spinnaker is in the windward bag, you may have to hoist on the windward side. It's possible for the crew to bundle up the spinnaker and throw it round the front of the forestay, in the moment when the helm pulls on the halyard like fury. The wind should blow it out to the leeward side, while the crew attaches the pole and sets the guy.

Hoisting the kite while sailing deep downwind. The helm steers with her legs and pulls the halyard hand-over-hand, leaving the crew free to fix the pole.

Trimming a symmetric spinnaker

- The guy is used to set the spinnaker's position at right angles to the wind, with the end of the pole pulled hard against the windward clew of the sail.

- The uphaul/downhaul adjusts pole height to ensure that both corners of the sail are level, which will provide optimum performance and control. When the spinnaker is set, the guy can be locked in its cleat.

- Sailing on a dead run, the pole needs to be pulled right back with the spinnaker flying high on the windward side. This ensures that both spinnaker and mainsail are driving the boat downwind. For perfect trim, the helm will sit to leeward by the boom with the crew slightly forward on the windward side. The end of the pole will need to be lowered to keep both corners of the spinnaker level.

- Sailing on a reach, the boom needs to be eased right forward, but do not let it press hard against the forestay. With a lot more lateral power, both crews will need to be on the windward side, with the crew hiking or out on the trapeze. The end of the pole should be raised to keep both corners level. Use a reaching hook or twinning line to pull the guy down to the shroud plate. This will ensure you can hike or trapeze, without being obstructed by the guy. It will also help to reduce the guy stretching under load.

- For maximum power, trim the spinnaker sheet until the luff is starting to fold inwards. Over-sheeting will reduce power in the sail. Ease the spinnaker sheet to check pole height. The luff should fold in the middle and peel towards the head and foot. If it peels from the top to the bottom, pole height needs adjusting.

Sailing dead downwind, the crew sits to windward and helm to leeward to balance the boat.

Gybing the spinnaker

Gybing a symmetric spinnaker is considerably more complex and slower than gybing an asymmetric. The gybing arc is also much smaller when gybing downwind on a running course to the leeward mark. The standard method of gybing the spinnaker is to physically move the pole from side to side, while the boat is sailing almost directly downwind. The helm needs to follow the spinnaker through the arc of the gybe, while balancing the boat to prevent it heeling.

1. Pull back on the guy to keep the spinnaker square to the wind as the boat steers into the gybe.

2. Flick the main boom across the new side, as the pole is unclipped from the mast and clipped on to the new guy. If you have problems getting the inner end of the pole off the mast, ease off downhaul tension. It will also be easier if the clip faces upwards, allowing the inner end to be pulled down.

3. Unclip the outer end of the pole from the old guy, which will take over as the new sheet.

4. Clip the end of the pole to the mast.

5. Pull the pole back to the correct position and trim the sheet.

• If you are gybing in stronger winds, both twinning lines can be pulled down to depower the spinnaker during the transition to the new gybe. Alternatively, the helm can stall the spinnaker behind the mainsail by pulling back on the sheet and guy.

• An experienced helm may steer through the gybe with the tiller between his legs, which leaves hands free to trim the sheet and guy for the crew while the crew concentrates on moving the pole to the new side. Alternatively, the sheet and guy could be cleated during the gybe. Different techniques will suit different boats and crews.

• If you are gybing from a reach to a reach, the gybing angle will be wider and the spinnaker will need to be pulled much further round the forestay.

Going for the gybe. The helm steers with her legs, leaving her hands free to hold the sheet and guy. The crew unclips the pole from the mast. She will clip it to the guy on the new side, unclip the old guy and clip the new inner end of the pole to the mast.

Dropping the spinnaker

- When possible, sail deep downwind to blanket the spinnaker.

- If the boat is fitted with a chute in the bows, let go the halyard, pull in the retrieval line, then unclip and pull the pole back alongside the boom.

- If the boat has a cockpit bag, the drop will be easiest on the windward side. Take the pole off the mast while continuing to fly the spinnaker on the final approach to the leeward mark. Pull the pole back alongside the boom and let go the halyard. Haul down on the leech, which will stretch the foot of the sail across the foredeck and prevent it dragging over the side, as the spinnaker is bundled into the windward side bag. Do not pull both clews together while dragging down the spinnaker, as this will tend to create twists.

Don't leave it too late to drop the kite. This Lark is having a spot of trouble, having run out of water during the Frensham Frenzy. They got the kite down without hitting the bank!

The joy of blasting. Many racers assume that symmetric kites are much smaller than asymmetrics. That's not true when 505 sailors have 27 square metres to play with!

30 Champion Advice

How do you sail quickest round the course? We asked five champion sailors from a variety of popular classes to provide their top tips for race winners ...

Steve Cockerill

Founder of Rooster Sailing and star of Boat Whisperer DVD videos. Laser Radial World Masters Champion 4 times; Laser Radial National Champion 8 times; Europe National Champion 7 times; RS300 National Champion 6 times; Blaze National Champion 6 times; Streaker National Champion 2 times; Graduate National Champion 2 itimes; Rooster 8.1 National Champion 1 time.

What is the most important thing you can do...

When setting up the boat before the race?

Make careful pre-race gear checks to ensure that ropes, bolts and pins are all safe and nothing will break. You should also set up the rig for the conditions, having checked the wind forecast.

In the 15 minutes before the start?

Check wind and current. If you have time, sail the whole course, but you must at least spot the buoys. Take transits early and sail the first beat to get an idea of wind cycles. Make a plan before you start!

In the last minute before the start?

Perfect positioning is what counts most. Slowly moving forward, always think about your positioning for the start.

In the first minute after the start?

Sail high and fast off the line, then just sail fast.

On the first windward leg?

Use the shifts as best you can. Consider if your plan has changed.

To maximise speed when sailing upwind?

Keep the boat upright and concentrate on boat trim.

On the final approach to the windward mark?

Keep things simple. Stay to the right of your closest opposition to gain the advantage of starboard tack.

On the turn round the windward mark or spacer mark?

Let the sail out, which sounds simple but it's important to get it right.

On the downwind leg?

Look for gusts to take best advantage.

To maximise speed when sailing downwind?

Concentrate on boat trim.

On the final approach to the leeward mark?

Keep it simple. Break all inside overlaps.

On the turn round the leeward mark?

Weight to leeward to help the boat turn fast.

On the final beat?

Keep between your opposition and the finish line.

On the approach to the finish line?

Check for bias – aim to finish at the closest end.

After the race?

Re-hydrate, eat and enjoy the after race banter. Don't forget to re-check your gear before the next day's racing.

Phil Sparks

Optimist National Champion in 2006 and Volvo ISAF Youth World 420 Champion 2009

Top tips for winning a race...

Get a good enough start. Be conservative and consider the fleet. Don't think about winning until you've won.
Get your priorities right. Boat speed. Be dynamic. Be consistent. Don't give up. Think about what is important at the time. Think fast.

Top tips for winning a regatta...

Be consistent – don't go for the win, go for the top 5. Always play the majorities. Keep a cool head. Plan before each race. Prioritise.

Andy Davis

Leading development class sailmaker with Speed Sails. Solo National Champion in a 90 boat fleet at Paignton in 2007 and top ranked Merlin Rocket helm.

What is the most important thing you can do...

When setting up the boat before the race?

I always start off by looking at the foils and hull first to make sure it's clean, polished and free of any chips or indentations. Next look at the rig. Make sure your settings – rake, rig tension and pre-bend – are correct for the boat and the conditions. Then make sure all your controls are working correctly and efficiently. If any blocks, cleats, ropes or shackles look like they could fail, make sure they are changed straight away. There should be no chance of having gear failure on the race course. Good preparation is the key to success.

In the 30 minutes before the start?

It is certainly worth spending time out on the race course to gain information to provide some good advantages. At any major championship, I always like to be the first boat off the slipway. You've got to watch what's happening. Going into the last race at the Solo nationals, the tide was very high and you could only launch one Solo at a time. I made sure I was first to launch to reduce the stress of making the start on time.

Before the start, I like to sail upwind and write down the numbers off the compass, which ensures I will know straight away whether I'm on a lifter or a header off the start line. Spend a bit of time looking upwind to find out where the bands of wind pressure are coming down the race course. Consider a nearby headland may cause wind bends and don't forget to assess the tide.

Once you are happy with the information you've gained, spend at least 10 minutes on the start line looking at line bias and deciding which end of the line you are going to start. Make transits for your position on the line. Allow plenty of time for all this – it's not helpful to rush your pre-start procedure.

In the last minute before the start?

I try to make sure I'm positioned in the place I want to start from on the line, and have also worked a nice gap to leeward so I can bear off and accelerate just before the start. I always make sure that no one can try to roll me with their dirty wind. If boats around me start going, then I must start going with them – you don't want to get stuck in the pack behind.

In the first minute after the start?

There is a lot to concentrate on immediately after the start. In the Solo I have to watch all the boats around me, while sailing my boat as fast as it will go upwind and maintaining my pointing ability. But in the Merlin I can concentrate on keeping the boat up to speed, while my crew relays information on what the other boats are doing.

On the first windward leg?

My tactics on the first windward leg can be quite different, depending on whether the wind is a steady breeze or very shifty. At the Solo nationals in Paignton, the wind was very shifty so it paid to sail up the middle of the course, tacking on the shifts rather than hitting the corners and having possible chances of big gains or big losses. At Pwllhelli in the Merlin nationals it was very different. The wind was much more predictable, so it was better to go out to the sides of the race course to make your gains. The tide also played a large role at that event.

To maximise speed when sailing upwind?

The best technique to maximise speed upwind is to try and keep a consistent heel on the boat. If you are able to keep the boat flat at all times, then the flow of air across your sail will become much more efficient, and the same applies for the flow of water across your centreboard. Increased efficiency from your sail and foils can provide a large increase in boat speed.

Another key factor for sailing upwind is, make sure the rig is set correctly. You don't want to be sailing upwind in Force 5 when your rig is set up for Force 2! Always take note of your rig set-up so you can gain the best speed out of your sails for any conditions.

On the final approach to the windward mark?

I hope to have worked myself into a position where I can round as close to the windward mark as possible, approaching on the lay line and making sure I'm not in any dirty air, which could lose me height. Once I'm feeling comfortable about coming up to the windward mark, I have a good look for where the next mark is so I can prepare to either attack any boats ahead or defend what I have gained from the upwind leg.

On the turn round the windward mark or spacer mark?

When bearing away round the windward mark, the boat must be kept flat – not only to maximise speed, but also to keep control. However a little heel to windward will also help the boat to bear away. Immediately after the bear-away I start to set the boat up for offwind. I'll know exactly where the next mark is, having spotted it while sailing up on the beat, so I can concentrate on getting the boat moving as fast as possible.

On the downwind leg?

Depending on what boats around me are doing, I like to work my boat as low as possible on this leg, which will ensure I'm coming up to the gybe mark or leeward mark with speed. The best way to gain this depth is by going down in the gusts and coming up in the lulls, in order to keep the boat traveling at a faster pace. Always try to make sure that no one is blanketing you downwind and keep clear air. If there are boats close by, they will try to sail over you.

To maximise speed when sailing downwind?

Keeping the boat flat is a good start. If you're sailing on a dead run, trying to find neutral helm works best. You can then use the heel of the boat to steer downwind, instead of a lot of rudder movement, which will act as a big brake.

On the final approach to the leeward mark?

When getting close to the leeward mark, judge how long you will need to get the boat ready for the next leg in preparation for a perfect mark rounding. Make sure you are on the inside of any boats on the run-up to the mark, and

that you will have an overlap on them to gain water by the two boat length rule. Check where the next mark of the course is, so you know your options on rounding the leeward mark. For instance, realising you must tack straight away could gain a lot of places or distance.

On the turn round the leeward mark?

I like to heel to leeward rounding the mark, which helps by using less rudder. Once round the mark, you can then bring the boat flat and need to put the rig back on its upwind settings as quickly as possible. Look at the compass and your numbers to work out if the wind direction has shifted.

On the final beat?

Not only are you still trying to get a bigger lead, or attempting to pass as many boats as possible, but you must also be sure to minimise threats from behind. Covering rival boats can be the key to a successful last beat.

On the approach to the finish line?

Try to work out if the committee boat or pin end is closest as soon as possible. You can then work your tactics towards the favoured end.

After the race?

I like to give myself a little de-brief, think about the good and bad parts of the race and consider what I can improve for the next race. Check wear and tear on your boat to make sure everything is working as it should. I always have a black chinagraph pencil in the boat. This allows me to write quick notes on the decks for whatever reason. Once that item has been ticked off, it will rub off easily!

Nick Craig

OK World Champion 3 times, Enterprise World Champion 1 time, RS 400 National Champion 2 times, Endeavour Trophy Champion 3 times.

What is the most important thing you can do…

When setting up the boat before the race?

I'm really bad at forgetting key things, such as my lunch! So I actually keep a list of everything I need for a day's racing and run through it before going sailing at big events. It's pretty tedious – only really worth bothering for major races!

In the 15 minutes before the start?

Check out the wind patterns to see if anything new has happened and whether line bias is still the same. You also need to check if the race officer does anything odd, like move the start line at the last minute.

In the last minute before the start?

Look to create a gap on the start line, so you have room to accelerate out of the start.

In the first minute after the start?

Hopefully look to consolidate a good position, which will let you tack to get across the fleet or sail free to drive over the fleet. But if you've got a bad start, you should be looking for a clear wind lane urgently!

On the first windward leg?

You need to keep an idea of how the fleet is distributed. Look to play the percentages, tending towards the side that you think is favoured, but not doing anything radical. By this I mean keep roughly half the fleet to the left of you and half the fleet to the right of you, relative to the windward mark. But if you think one side is likely to pay, you can shift that way. If you feel like a gamble, you could even go all the way to having the whole fleet on one side!

To maximise speed when sailing upwind?

Smooth steering through the waves can make a big difference.

On the final approach to the windward mark?

Don't try to do anything too clever, such as come in on port tack or nail the lay line with an inch to spare. Just being sensible often results in a place gain or two.

On the turn round the windward mark or spacer mark?

Before you get there, get an idea of which way you want to go – high/low or left/right – and be proactive about it. Being caught in the middle downwind generally doesn't pay.

On the downwind leg?

Good wave steering in clear water is the key to offwind speed.

On the approach to the leeward mark?

Think early about which side the inside overlap will be and work towards establishing it. Leeward mark roundings are generally to port, so you are looking to get on the left of the

pack in the late stages of a run, or high of the pack in the late stages of a reach. If the mark is a starboard rounding, the approach will be reversed.

On the turn round the leeward mark?

You should already have a plan for the next beat which will dictate how you turn. If you're looking to carry on, then you will need a clear lane on that tack. If you're looking to tack, a more aggressive rounding can be made without worrying about clear wind, because you're about to tack off anyway.

On the final beat?

Assess where you are in relation to your overall goal for that race. If you are behind, be more aggressive in going towards the side of the beat you think is paying. If you are ahead, cover the pack whilst tending towards the favoured side.

On the approach to the finish line?

Know upfront which end of the line is biased. If the finish line is the same as the start line, bias will be the opposite way round.

After the race?

Refuel quickly to keep energy levels up. Don't miss any of the basics (as I often have!) such as signing in to show you have correctly finished the race.

The Endeavour Trophy

First raced in 1961, the Endeavour Trophy is the 'Championship of Champions' for current national champions in up to 30 dinghy classes. It is a weekend event at the end of the season, raced in a fleet of identical boats provided specially for the championship – recent choices have included the RS400 and Topaz Xenon. The Endeavour Trophy itself is a superb scale model of the J-Class yacht Endeavour, originally donated by Beecher Moore who was a business partner to dinghy designer Jack Holt.

Frances Peters

29er National Youth Champion with Hannah Diamond; 29er European Championships with Hannah Diamond – 1st European Girls; RS Feva European and National Champion with Claire Lasko.

What is the most important thing you can do...

When setting up the boat before the race?

Check everything over. In particular, make sure the kite's rigged correctly and that nothing's going to break while you're racing.

In the 15 minutes before the start?

Before you leave the beach, arrange to sail upwind and downwind with another boat, to check your speed. Think about what your priorities are going to be. Is the course going to be shifty and gusty? Is there any way to make obvious gains? For instance, one side of the course may have better wind or tide.

In the last minute before the start?

Make sure you're just where you want to be, both on the line and in relation to other boats. Focus on keeping in the front row, preferably in a position that's hidden from the committee boat by other people's sails. Always work on creating a gap to leeward, so you can go full bore with the start signal.

In the first minute after the start?

Sail flat out and focus 100% on holding your lane. Don't look around at other boats too much. Just be aware of what's happening with any boats that are close, while footing to windward as fast as you can!

On the first windward leg?

Keep clear wind, sail with the lifts and try to link the gusts into a pattern which gets you closer to the windward mark. If you're not sailing fast enough to keep pace with other sailors, try going into a little mental bubble for about a minute, in which nothing else exists except you and the boat. Make sure only one person in the boat is looking around at any given time – you don't need two people to watch what's happening on the course.

On the final approach to the windward mark?

Make sure you're not going to get stuck below the starboard lay line, with no gap to tack into which would be a disaster. Try to keep mark roundings as simple as possible. Before you get there, start thinking about which way you think will pay best downwind. Work out if the spinnaker hoist will be a straight set (same tack hoist) or gybe set (gybing during the hoist). Consider what the fleet is doing so you can be sure to keep clear wind.

On the downwind leg?

Don't chase the gusts and don't head for gusts you're not going to get! If you're leading, stay between the fleet and the leeward mark. If you're attacking from behind, try and split from the main bunch of boats – you can take a few more risks.

To maximise speed when sailing downwind?

Be dynamic! Keep moving to catch the waves and synchronise pumping of the mainsail and kite with crew movement fore and aft. How you do this will depend on the gusts and waves.

On the final approach to the leeward mark?

If you're defending from ahead, keep your rounding simple and make a straight drop. If you're attacking from behind, consider if a last minute gybe-drop might pay, but always try to get the inside overlap within two boat lengths of the mark. On some courses there is a leeward gate, in which case you need to assess which mark is biased by being a little further upwind. Always go 'in wide out tight'. It's vital to keep height out of the mark, so you can hold your windward lane.

On the final beat?

If you're attacking, split away from the fleet by tacking off when you can and hope to make some gains. If you're defending, always stay between the fleet and the finish line. Guard against a situation where another boat could overtake on a favourable wind shift. As you approach the line, decide which end is biased in your favour. If you are still attacking or defending, a starboard approach may be the winning choice.

After the race?

Discuss with your crew or coach what worked and what didn't during the race. Pick out the good points of the race and bank them, then set a goal for the next race.

31 The Beaufort Scale

Admiral Sir Francis Beaufort, who lived from 1774-1857, is widely credited with the invention of the Beaufort Scale in 1806 while serving on board HMS Woolwich. In times long before reliable anemometers, it was used to help sailors estimate wind strength by matching the appearance of the open sea against a list of careful descriptions. It seems likely that similar scales of wind force were in use many years before Admiral Beaufort was even born, but the immortal Admiral still gets all the credit! In modern times, the Beaufort Scale is still widely used for maritime weather forecasts and quoted by dinghy sailors and yachtsmen as the official gauge of the wind.

Force	Knots	Mph	Km/h	Description	Effects at sea	Effects on land
0	0-1	0	0	Calm	Sea like a mirror	Smoke rises vertically

No use for racing. Wait on beach and make sure your boat is perfectly prepared.

Force	Knots	Mph	Km/h	Description	Effects at sea	Effects on land
1	1-3	1-3	1-6	Light air	Ripples, but no foam crests	Smoke drifts in the wind

Drifting round the course, with the crew sitting right forward to lift the stern and the boat heeled to leeward to put some shape in the sails. If conditions continue like this, the organisers will shorten the race

Force	Knots	Mph	Km/h	Description	Effects at sea	Effects on land
2	4-6	4-7	7-11	Light breeze	Small wavelets but crests do not break	Leaves rustle. Wind felt on face

The boat will pick up a little speed and may heel slightly to leeward – enough for a dinghy crew to sit up on the windward side.

Force	Knots	Mph	Km/h	Description	Effects at sea	Effects on land
3	7-10	8-12	12-19	Gentle breeze	Large wavelets with a few white horses	Small twigs in constant motion. Light flags extended

The start of a good racing breeze. Hike upwind to hold the fuller powered boat upright. Skiffs will start to plane.

Force	Knots	Mph	Km/h	Description	Effects at sea	Effects on land
4	11-15	13-18	20-29	Moderate breeze	Small waves with fairly frequent white horses	Dust, leaves and loose paper raised. Small branches move

Perfect conditions for racing. Dinghy crews will be fully extended, hiking or on the trapeze, with the rig depowered upwind and fast planing offwind.

Force	Knots	Mph	Km/h	Description	Effects at sea	Effects on land
5	16-21	19-24	30-39	Fresh breeze	Moderate waves with many white horses	Small trees sway

Great conditions for dinghy racing if you have the technique to handle a flat out blast round the course. Most boats will be well overpowered. Rescue boats will get busy with capsizes.

Force	Knots	Mph	Km/h	Description	Effects at sea	Effects on land
6	22-27	25-31	40-50	Strong breeze	Larger waves form with white foam crests and some spray	Large branches are swaying. Umbrellas are used with difficulty

You need to be very good to get round the course in this much wind, though racing is perfectly possible in sheltered water with reliable safety back up.

Force	Knots	Mph	Km/h	Description	Effects at sea	Effects on land
7	28-33	32-38	51-62	Near gale	Sea heaps up with white foam blown in streaks along the waves	Inconvenience felt when walking against the wind with whole trees swaying

Racing is cancelled. If dinghies are caught out on the course, the result could be carnage!

RYA Laser Handbook

RYA G53

By Paul Goodison

Fantastic book by Britain's top rated Laser sailor who raced at the Olympics in 2008. Not only all you need to know about sailing and racing a Laser, but also lots of useful tips and information for dinghy racers in general. Highly recommended.

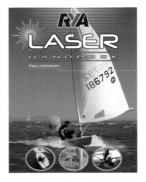

RYA Racing Rules of Sailing

RYA YR1/2009-2012

The complete Racing Rules of Sailing including RYA Prescriptions. This 186-page booklet is published in an easy-to-use, spiral bound, pocket size format.

RYA Crew to Win

RYA G39

By Joe Glanfield

Joe Glanfield progressed from crewing a Cadet at the age of 9 to winning a Silver Medal at the 2004 Olympics, crewing a 470 with Nick Rogers. This book is a mine of information on racing a trapeze boat with a symmetrical spinnaker, plus there's a small 49er section to keep skiff racers happy.

RYA Handy Guide to the Racing Rules

RYA YR 2009-2012

Most dinghy racers will never need to consult the complete Racing Rules. This little booklet summarises all you need to know to handle most situations, with easy-to-understand full colour illustrations to explain each major rule. What's more, it's printed on tough coated paper. Every racer should have a copy!

RYA Tactics   RYA G40

By Mark Rushall

You not only have to sail the boat perfectly, you also have to be a cunning mastermind. Mark Rushall unravels and explains all the complexities of tactical sailing. This impressive book is without doubt the definitive tactical bible and provides a huge amount of information with great illustrations.

RYA Youth & Junior Racing Guide

This 56-page booklet provides a complete guide to youth and junior racing administered by the RYA. Information includes Squad Programmes and Pathways, Case Studies of sailors, specifications of Junior and Youth Classes, Coaching and the Volvo RYA Champion Club Programme. **FREE!** email: amy.packard@rya.org.uk

RYA Catamaran Handbook   RYA G46

By Jeremy Evans

Fancy racing a catamaran? Jeremy Evans explains all you need to know about sailing on two hulls, with the accent firmly on racing Tigers, F18s, Hobie 16s and other high performance cats.

RYA Optimist Handbook

RYA G44

By Alan Williams

All you ever wanted to know about racing Optimists and a lot more! A superb book packed full of information for Oppie racers and their parents.

Apparent wind The wind when you are moving.
Asymmetric A spinnaker with longer luff than leech, also known as a 'gennaker.'
Back Wind rotating anti-clockwise, against the sun.
Backed A sail filled in the reverse direction. The jib 'backs' to help pull the bows round when tacking.
Balance Holding the boat upright and level.
Barber hauler Control to adjust horizontal sheeting angle of jib.
Bearing away Turning away from the wind
Beaufort Scale Traditional wind speed indicator.
Black Flag Any boat OCS within 1 minute of the start is disqualified.
Blanketing During a spinnaker hoist or drop, the spinnaker is protected (blanketed) by the mainsail.
Centreboard Main foil which swivels up and down inside case.
Centre of Effort Main fulcrum of power in sails.
Centre of Lateral Resistance Where boat turns about centreboard/daggerboard.
Chute Tubular chute which stores the spinnaker in the foredeck. Can be a cloth sock or solid chute built into the bows.
Class Flag Displays which class is about to start the race.
Clew Back corner of sail.
Code Flag I Any boat OCS within 1 minute of the start must go round the ends to restart.
Code Flag P Preparatory flag for a race.
Code Flag X Individual recall.
Code Flag Z Any boat OCS within 1 minute of the start will have its score reduced by 20% penalty.
Committee Boat Start boat at starboard end of the line.
Covering Sitting on another boat so it is stuck in your dirty wind and cannot escape by 'breaking cover'.
Cunningham Control line used to tension luff of mainsail.
Dacron Woven sail material.
Daggerboard Main foil which lifts vertically up and down.
DSQ Disqualified.
Epoxy Top quality resin for strong and light dinghy hulls.
First Substitute Flag General recall.

Foam sandwich Hull construction using lightweight foam core between inner and outer skins which are generally glass fibre, although materials such as carbon fibre may be used. Provides optimum stiffness and light weight.
Foils Rudder blades, daggerboards and centreboards.
Foot Bottom of a sail.
Forestay Front wire which holds up the mast. Many dinghies incorporate forestay inside jib luff.
Gnav Strut which pushes down on boom, providing same function as kicking strap.
Gradient Wind Wind due to weather systems, not local effects.
Gudgeons Brackets for rudder pintles.
Gybing Changing tacks with the wind behind.
Head Top of a sail.
Headboard Reinforced top of mainsail.
Header Wind shift taking your further from an upwind mark, or closer to a downwind mark.
Hikers Shorts worn when hiking.
Hiking Leaning over side decks to balance boat.
High 'Going high' or 'luffing' is sailing towards the wind.
Inner distance mark Buoy marking end of start line next to committee boat.
Kicking Strap Rope or wire control used to pull down the boom and manage the amount of twist in the mainsail. Also known as 'kicker' or 'vang.'
Kite Euphemism for spinnaker.
Larks foot Rope looped through itself. A double larks foot can be used to attach sheets securely to the clew of a jib or asymmetric spinnaker.
Lay line Imaginary line along which you can sail to the windward mark without tacking.
Leech Trailing edge of sail.
Leeward The direction in which the wind is blowing.
Leeward boat A boat downwind.
Leeward mark Bottom of the race course.
Leeway Being pushed sideways by the wind.
Lift Wind shift taking you closer to an upwind mark, or further from a downwind mark.

Line Bias When the start line (or finish line) is not perfectly at right angles to the wind.
Low 'Going low' is sailing away from the wind.
Lowers Lower shrouds to control mast bend.
Luff Leading edge of sail.
Luffing Turning towards the wind.
Mast Rake Angle of mast from vertical.
Mast Ram Used to control lower bend in mast.
Mylar Laminate material mainly used for mainsails. Very resistant to stretch under load.
Neap Tides Period of month when tidal range is smallest.
OCS On Course Side. Over the line at the start.
One Design A dinghy class in which all boats are the same.
Ooching Rocking your body to propel the boat.
OOD Officer of the Day.
Outer Distance Mark Far end of the start line from the committee boat.
Outhaul Control for tensioning foot of the sail.
Overlap When part of a boat overlaps part of another boat.
Penalty 360 or 720 turn to make good a racing rule infringement.
Pin end Port end of the start line – the leeward end when the fleet starts on starboard tack.
Pinching Squeezing very close the the wind on a beat.
Pintles Steel pins for attaching rudder stock to gudgeons.
Planing Skimming over surface of water on bow wave. This provides a substantial boost in speed over displacement sailing through the water.
Pointing Pointing towards the wind while sailing fast on a beat.
Port Left.
Port Tack Sailing with the wind on the port side.
Protests Used when an infringement of the racing rules is contested.
Pumping Moving the sheet rapidly in and out to power the sail.
Rhumb line Imaginary straight line between two marks.
Rip Stop Lightweight nylon for spinnakers.
Rocker Longitudinal curve in the hull shape. More rocker helps the boat turn faster.
Roll tack A rolling tack which fans the sails for increased drive.
Sailing Instructions Written information on the race format.

Shrouds Side wires which hold up the mast.
Slot Area of windflow between mainsail and jib.
Spreaders Horizontal struts to control mast bend.
Spring Tides Period in month when tidal range is greatest.
Starboard Right.
Starboard Tack Sailing with the wind on the starboard side.
Tack Front corner of a sail.
Tacking Changing tacks with the wind ahead.
Telltales Wool or plastic strips which show how air is flowing across the sails.
Tidal range Difference between high and low water.
Transom Flat back at the stern.
Trapeze Wire for the crew to hang off the mast.
Traveller Slider which allows the mainsheet to be pulled to the windward side.
Trim Fore and aft adjustment of crew weight in boat.
Transit Two fixed objects in line.
True Wind The wind when you are stationary.
Twist The shape of the mainsail or jib when seen from astern. Twist in the top of the sail is used to reduce power upwind.
Veer The wind rotates clockwise or in the same direction as the sun.
Water Room needed at a mark or obstruction.
Weather helm Boat has a tendency to steer upwind. Slight weather helm is normally desirable.
Wing-wang Control to pull spinnaker pole to windward side of bows.
Wind bend Wind shift that increases as you sail into it.
Wind shadow Sails affected by turbulence from nearby sails. Also known as 'dirty wind.'
Wind Shift A change in wind direction, which may necessitate a tack or gybe in order to sail higher or lower towards the next mark.
Windward The side the wind is blowing from.
Windward boat A boat upwind.
Windward mark Top of the race course.
Windward-Leeward Course A sausage-shaped racing course with just two legs, directly upwind and downwind.

34 | Useful Web Addresses

Organisations

www.rya.org	Royal Yachting Association (RYA)
www.sailing.org	International Sailing Federation (ISAF)
www.teamracing.org.uk	United Kingdom Team Racing Association
www.skandiateamgbr.com	Official website for British Sailing Team in Olympic and Paralympic Classes
www.wpnsa.org.uk	Weymouth and Portland National Sailing Academy

Weather

www.windguru.cz	Popular weather forecast website for sailing and windsurfing.
www.metoffice.gov.uk/weather/marine/inshore_forecast.html	Detailed forecast for inshore waters around the UK.
www.xcweather.co.uk	Designed for aircraft, but provides detailed information on forecast wind speed and direction across the UK.

Index

Index